02114767

KT-514-210

THE ROUGH GUIDE to

iPods, iTunes
& music online

4th Edition

ROUGH GUIDES

www.roughguides.com

RODE'S COLLEGE LIBRARY

Credits

**The Rough Guide to iPods, iTunes
& Music Online**

Text, design and layout:
Peter Buckley and Duncan Clark
Proofreading: Anna Leggett
Production: Aimee Hampson

Rough Guides Reference

Series editor: Mark Ellingham
Editors: Peter Buckley, Duncan Clark,
Tracy Hopkins, Sean Mahoney,
Matt Milton, Joe Staines, Ruth Tidball
Director: Andrew Lockett

Publishing Information

This fourth edition published September 2006 by
Rough Guides Ltd, 80 Strand, London WC2R 0RL
345 Hudson St, 4th Floor, New York 10014, USA
Email: mail@roughguides.com

Distributed by the Penguin Group:

Penguin Books Ltd, 80 Strand, London WC2R 0RL
Penguin Putnam, Inc., 375 Hudson Street, NY 10014, USA
Penguin Group (Australia), 250 Camberwell Road, Camberwell, Victoria 3124, Australia
Penguin Books Canada Ltd, 10 Alcorn Avenue, Toronto, Ontario, Canada M4P 2Y3
Penguin Group (New Zealand), 67 Apollo Drive, Mairangi Bay, Auckland 1310, New Zealand

Printed in Italy by LegoPrint S.p.A.

Typeset in Minion and Myriad to an original design by Peter Buckley and Duncan Clark

The publishers and authors have done their best to ensure the accuracy and currency of all information
in The Rough Guide to iPods, iTunes & Music Online; however, they can accept no responsibility for any
loss or inconvenience sustained by any reader as a result of its information or advice.

No part of this book may be reproduced in any form without permission from the publisher except for
the quotation of brief passages in reviews.

© Peter Buckley and Duncan Clark, 2006

272 pages; includes index

A catalogue record for this book is available from the British Library

ISBN 13: 978-1-84353-727-4
ISBN 10: 1-84353-727-3

1 3 5 7 9 8 6 4 2

THE ROUGH GUIDE to

iPods, iTunes
& music online

written by
Peter Buckley and Duncan Clark

ROUGH
GUIDES

RODE'S COLLEGE
LIBRARY

www.roughguides.com

Contents

Music online

More than music

Extras

First aid

iPodology

Introduction

why a book about iPods and iTunes?

When we first thought of writing this book, we wondered whether there would be enough to say. Apple are famous for making user-friendly products, and iPods and iTunes are particularly intuitive. But once we started talking to people who either already had an iPod or were thinking of buying one, we realized there was clearly a need. Everyone had a question – "Is the sound quality any good?", "How do I move music between my two computers?", "AAC or MP3?", "Is downloading illegal?"…

So here are a couple of hundred pages of answers, not only covering iPod and iTunes basics, but everything from finding music online and choosing the right audio file formats to resurrecting your old vinyl collection and getting it into your pocket. You'll also find a few samples of iPod culture – such as the devoted fans who obsess about their Pods' names and photograph the world reflected in their gadgets' mirrored backs. Not everyone is quite that keen, of course, but one thing that all Pod users agree on is that iPods change our relationship with music. And with the scores of tips and tricks provided in this book, that relationship should be as satisfying as a Bach fugue. Or a Coltrane solo. Or a Missy Elliott acappella…

Note!

Each new version of iTunes brings a different set of features, and each new iPod model works slightly differently.

This book was written using iTunes 6.0.4, so if you have something older, be sure to upgrade to the most recent version (see p.40) or many of the functions covered here will be missing. Likewise, if you have something newer (iTunes updates are released every few months), expect to find numerous extras.

As for hardware, this book focuses on the models available in June 2006: the video iPod, the iPod nano and the iPod shuffle. Most of what we say will apply to older models, too, though certain features – Notes, Dock connectors, and so on – were only introduced with the third-generation iPods in 2003.

Basics & buying

01

iPods &
digital
music

everything you ever wanted
to know but were afraid to ask

This book should help you get the best from an iPod, from iTunes and from online music. However, before we get into the nitty-gritty of everything from ripping tracks from vinyl to using the iPod as a hard drive, let's address all those general questions that you've probably already asked yourself (and some that you probably haven't) about the world of MP3 players and digital music. You'll find more details on many of these subjects later on.

Basics

basics & buying

What is an iPod?

An iPod is like a cross between a Walkman and the hard drive used to store files in a computer. Instead of playing from cassettes, CDs or other media, an iPod holds music internally as digital data, in just the same way as a computer stores word-processing documents and other files.

iPods aren't unique in this respect: many devices do roughly the same thing. They're collectively known as digital music players or (for reasons soon to be explained) MP3 players. But the iPod – produced by Apple, best known for their Mac range of computers – is currently by far the most popular of the numerous brands on the market.

Hard drives and flash

High-capacity digital music players, including the full-size iPod, store their music on a hard drive, or "hard disk" – just like the one found in a standard home computer, but a bit smaller. Lower-capacity digital music players, however – such as the iPod nano and iPod shuffle – store their music using something known as "flash memory": tiny chips of the kind found in digital-camera memory cards. Hard drives can store much more music and other files but flash memory is much smaller physically and more resistant to being knocked around.

What's so good about digital music players?

There are numerous attractions in putting your music on an iPod or other high-spec digital music player. Compared to other types of personal stereo, they win hands down. For one thing, they can store a huge quantity of music – thousands of albums in some cases – so you can listen to whatever you want, wherever you are. Secondly, since there are no CDs or tapes to carry about, all you have to take with you is a small, self-contained device. Furthermore, digital music players (like other personal stereos) can be hooked up to home hi-fis or car stereos, which means you can have your entire music collection instantly accessible at home, at friends' houses, when you're driving – even on holiday.

What else can they do?

Besides being a record collection on the go, digital music players allow you to do numerous useful and interesting things. You can play tracks downloaded from the Internet, for example, without the hassle of burning a CD. You can instantly compile playlists of selected songs or albums: a four-hour upbeat selection for a party, say, or a shorter selection for a walk to work. Or have your player select your music for you, picking tracks randomly from across your whole collection or just from albums of a particular genre.

Any iPod with a colour screen will also allow you to display photos, and the latest full-size iPods even allow you to play video files. So you can have your digital photo albums with you at all times (a mixed blessing for friends and relatives, admittedly), as well as home movies and even copies of your DVDs (see p.179).

On top of all that, you can also use digital music players as portable hard drives to back up or transfer any kind of computer files. A 60GB iPod, for example, is the equivalent of roughly 45,000 floppy disks: enough to back up a huge quantity of documents, emails and photos. And most digital music players can also function as personal organizers – with electronic diaries, address books, musical alarm clocks, and so on – and even Dictaphones (see p.204).

Furthermore, digital music players can play audiobooks and other spoken-word recordings. Their large capacity makes it practical to store entire texts – so you don't have to make do with the hatchet-job abridgements typically found on cassettes and CDs.

And that's not all. Here are a few other things you can do with an iPod, some of which require a third-party accessory...

▶ **Record voice memos** (see p.204).

▶ **Read news and email on the train** (see p.224).

▶ **Use an iPod as a universal remote control** (see p.219).

▶ **Download photos direct from your camera** (see p.210).

▶ **Navigate the road network** (see p.228).

▶ **Interrupt an FM radio signal with a DIY newsflash** (see p.206).

▶ **Deliver a PowerPoint presentation** (see p.178).

▶ **Automatically back up key files** (see p.231).

▶ **Play a few built-in games** (look within the Extras menu).

▶ **Make a flipbook movie** (see p.178).

▶ **Listen to poetry** (see p.164).

▶ **Shave off your beard** (see p.251).

Is an iPod the best digital music player to buy?

The various members of the iPod family are the best-known digital music players and they have much to recommend them. They're solidly built but small and light. They're very reliable and easy to use. They work with the excellent iTunes software (more on this below). There are scores of accessories and piles of extra software available for them. And they're masterpieces of ergonomic and aesthetic design (with the one exception of the grossly misjudged U2 special edition, released in late 2004). However, as with most Apple products, these qualities are reflected in the price.

There are many similar players which lack the wide reputation and minimalist design but which offer more features – such as an integrated radio, longer battery life, a bigger hard drive, the ability to record straight from a stereo rather than via a computer – for less money.

There are a growing number of brands on the market, but the field is still overwhelmingly dominated by Apple and a handful of competitors: Creative Labs (who produce the Zen brand), iRiver and Sony. From here on in, this book focuses exclusively on iPods;

Various devices, such as this Creative Portable Media Center, have been touted as "iPod killers", but so far none has made a really significant dent in the iPod's massive market share.

to get a sense of how the other brands compare, browse the selection and reviews at: www.amazon.com or www.amazon.co.uk

Can an iPod really hold my whole CD collection?

That depends on the model you buy, the sound quality you desire and – obviously – the size of your collection. The top-of-the-range iPod at the time of writing is capable of storing around 1300 albums at a sound quality that will satisfy most people: that's enough music to play day and night for more than a month without repeating a single track. So, assuming you own less music than that, you don't insist on super-high fidelity, and you're prepared to pay for a suitably capacious model, then yes, an iPod can hold your whole music collection. However, it's worth bearing in mind that in practice you also need the same amount of space available on the hard drive of your computer, since whatever is on your iPod will typically also live on your PC or Mac…

So I need a computer, too?

Yes – or at the very least you need access to one. For one thing, a computer is the only way to get music onto an iPod. To copy a CD onto an iPod, for example, you first copy it onto the computer (you "rip" the CD, to use the jargon) and then transfer it from the computer to the Pod. You can't cut out this step because the iPod has neither a CD drive nor the necessary processing power to extract the music directly. But even if you could cut out this step, it would still be better to combine your iPod with a computer. That way, you don't lose all your music and files if your iPod is lost, broken or stolen – you have a complete backup on your computer. Furthermore, a computer also allows you to download music from the Internet.

Is my current computer up to the job?

If you bought a PC or Mac in the last few years, it will probably be capable of working with an iPod, but it's certainly worth checking before blowing all your money. The box overleaf explains the minimum requirements and the upgrade options if your computer doesn't have what it takes.

What are iTunes and the iTunes Music Store?

iTunes is a piece of software, produced by Apple, for managing and playing music stored on your computer. It's also used for moving music from your computer to your iPod, but you don't *need* an iPod to use iTunes. If you're mainly interested in creating a digital music collection to listen to at home – rather than carry around with you – you can do this using iTunes. After all, your computer can do everything an iPod can do, including being hooked up to a hi-fi (see p.129).

Another function of the iTunes software is to provide access to the iTunes Music Store, which is one of various Internet-based services from which you can legally buy and download music. Currently the *only* way to access the Store is via iTunes: you can't shop there by visiting the Apple website using a regular Web browser. Note, though, that you don't have to buy music from the iTunes Music Store. You can use iTunes to play music copied from CD or other computers, or downloaded from elsewhere on the Internet (though music files from certain other online music stores may not be compatible).

There are many other programs similar to iTunes (but without the built-in iTunes Music Store access). They're collectively referred to as "jukeboxes". Though it is possible to use some iPods with a different jukebox program, there's currently not much reason why you'd want to.

basics & buying

Computer requirements & upgrade options

Any Mac or PC produced in the last couple of years, including laptops, should be fine for use with an iPod, and many older ones will also work. But it's certainly worth checking your hardware before buying a Pod. The core requirements are a recent operating system and the right socket to plug the iPod into. But you'll also need enough hard drive space to store your music, and, ideally, a fast Internet connection. Let's look at these four requirements in turn.

▶ **Windows XP (or 2000) or Mac OS X (v10.3 or later)** To check what operating system you have on a PC, right-click the My Computer icon and select Properties. If you have Windows Me or 98, you could consider upgrading to XP but you'll have to pay (around $95/£85); it can be a bit of a headache (some older programs and hardware don't work on XP); and you'll need to check whether your hardware is up to the job (see www.microsoft.com /windowsxp). If you have Windows 95, it's probably a matter of buying a new computer. Windows 2000 users should be OK, though you will need to make sure they have downloaded the latest updates from Microsoft via Windows Update in the Start menu.

On a Mac, select About This Mac or System Profiler from the Apple menu. If you have OS X v10.3 or later you'll be OK with any current iPod, though you might have to run the Software Update tool (also in the Apple menu) to grab the latest updates. OS X v10.2 will work with iPod shuffles and older iPod models only. If you have OS 9 or earlier, then no iPods will work.

Upgrading to the latest version of OS X costs around $130/£90. But first check the minimum requirements to make sure your machine could handle the new operating system (see www.apple.com/macosx).

▶ **USB** This is the computer "port" (socket) to which you connect a recent iPod. Any USB socket will work, though ideally you want USB2 (found on most PCs and Macs made after 2003), as this makes it more than ten times faster to transfer music and other data to the iPod than old-style USB (check your computer's manual, as USB and USB2 ports look identical).

If you don't have a USB2 port, you could add one to your computer by purchasing a suitable adapter. These are available for as little as $30/£20 for desktops and around double that for laptops. Or, if you have the right port but it's occupied by another device, buy a powered "hub" to turn a single port into two or more. These start at around $30/£20.

Note that most older full-size iPods and iPod minis can connect via FireWire (also known by the more prosaic title of IEEE1394) as well as USB.

▶ **Lots of hard drive space** It is possible to store more music on your iPod than on your computer, but it's *much* easier, more flexible and more secure to have your entire Music Library on both. So you ideally need at least as much free hard drive space as the size of the iPod you're planning on buying – and more if you're buying a small-capacity model. To find out how big and how full your hard drive is on a PC, open My Computer, right-click the C-drive icon and select Properties; on a Mac, single-click your hard drive icon on the Desktop or in a Finder window and select Get Info from the File menu. If you don't have enough space – bearing in mind that you can fit around fifteen to twenty albums on one gigabyte – try deleting any large files that you no longer need (or burning them to CDs) and then empty the Recycle Bin or Trash. On a PC, you could also try running the Disk Cleanup utility: right-click the C-drive icon, select Properties, and then press the Disk Cleanup button. If you still don't have enough space, consider adding an extra hard drive to your computer: these start at around $50/£30 for one that can be installed inside your computer's body, with higher-capacity and external drives (necessary for laptops) costing more.

▶ **An Internet connection** You can survive without this, but an Internet connection allows you to do clever things such as automatically add the track and artist names for all the music you copy from CD. It also allows you to download tracks from the Internet, though this can be frustratingly slow unless you have a broadband connection.

For everything you need to know about choosing, using and upgrading a PC, Mac or Internet connection, see this book's sister volumes: *The Rough Guide to PCs & Windows*, *The Rough Guide to Macs & OS X* and *The Rough Guide to the Internet*.

iPods work fine with laptops as well as desktops, and PCs as well as Macs

basics & buying

OK. Sounds good. But...

Isn't it a hassle to transfer all my music from CD to computer to iPod?

It certainly takes a while to transfer a large CD collection onto your computer, but not as long as it would take to play the CDs. Depending on your computer, it can take just a few minutes to transfer the contents of a CD onto your computer's hard drive – and you can listen to the music, or do some work in another application, while this is happening. Still, if you have more money than time, there are services that will take away your CDs and rip them into a well-organized collection for around $1/£1 per CD. See, for example:

PodServe www.podserve.co.uk (UK)
DMP3 www.dmp3music.com (US)
RipDigital www.ripdigital.com (US)

1. Place your order - we'll help.
2. FedEx your CDs to RipDigital - we supply packing materials and insurance.
3. Receive your digital music library - just plug it in and enjoy.

Once your music is on your PC or Mac, it only takes a matter of minutes to transfer even a large collection across to the iPod; and subsequent transfers from computer to iPod are even quicker, as only new or changed files are copied over.

I've heard the sound quality isn't great. Is that true?

Audiophiles sometimes turn their noses up at iPods and other digital music players on the grounds that the sound quality is not too hot. It's true that – at the default settings – the sound is marginally worse than CD, but you're unlikely to notice much (or any) difference unless you do a careful side-by-side comparison through a decent home stereo. Anyway, this sound quality isn't fixed. When you import tracks from CD (or record them from vinyl) you can choose from a wide range of options, up to and including full CD quality. The only problem is that better-quality recordings take up more disk space, which means fewer tracks on your iPod. Still, the trade-off between quality and quantity is entirely for you to decide upon. For more on this, see p.113.

What if my computer dies?

Hard drives occasionally give up the ghost, in which case the only chance of getting any of the contents back is a time-consuming and potentially expensive data-recovery process. And, of course, computers meet many other nasty ends: theft, lightning, spilled coffee and so on. If this happens, and you lose all the music stored on your PC or Mac's hard drive, it can be a real pain. However, with a little know-how (see p.222) it's possible to move all your music back from your iPod onto a new hard drive or computer (Apple tend to keep this relatively quiet, since it makes it very easy to illegally distribute your music collection onto your friends' computers). Obviously, however, you'll only be able to transfer what's on the iPod at that time, so if you don't keep your entire collection on both your computer and your iPod, it's definitely worth backing up your hard drive (see p.231).

What was that furore in the press about iPod batteries?

The current generation of iPods have rechargeable, lithium-ion batteries, much like the ones in laptop computers. After a full charge, which takes around three or four hours, they can play up to twenty hours of music (depending on the model: see p.26) and/or remain on standby for days. But, like all such batteries, they don't live forever. After 500 or so full recharges – which could be anywhere between two and ten years' usage – they start holding less and less power before eventually dying completely. When iPod users first realized this, they were shocked to learn that the battery was not user-replaceable and that to have it replaced by Apple would cost so much that they might as well bin the iPod and buy a new one. After much public pressure and a few legal threats, however, Apple dropped the price of the service to $99 in the US, and an equivalent amount elsewhere (still a lot, though no more than an average laptop battery). Since then, various third-party services have popped up offering a much cheaper "unofficial" service. If you look online, you'll also find batteries for sale, with instructions for doing it yourself. For more info, see p.240.

The Neistat Bros were so upset when they realized their iPod batteries were effectively non-replaceable that they felt compelled to make a film. Happily, the batteries can now be replaced for much less than the price of a new iPod.

Isn't this whole thing just another consumerist fad from a money-grabbing music industry?

The extraordinary range of music formats we've had in the last half-century – vinyl, cassette, CD, DAT, MiniDisc, SACD – has often been described as a cynical ploy by the music and electronics industries to make us buy ever more equipment and multiple copies of the same recordings. Whatever your view on this, digital music players such as the iPod are qualitatively different from the rest. For a start, they certainly weren't dreamed up by the music industry: in fact, the music industry is quaking in its boots about anything that combines music with computers, since the world of "digital music" makes it incredibly easy to illegally share copyrighted material – both via the Internet or simply by copying, say, 500 albums from a friend's computer in a matter of minutes.

As for whether iPods are another unnecessary consumer fad from the electronics industry is a matter for debate. True, they're ultimately expensive gadgets bought and designed by wealthy Westerners and manufactured in an oppressive regime where labour rights are poor (China). The same is true for much electronic equipment. But from an environmental perspective, at least, you can make a pretty strong case for a device that deals with music purely as digital data: downloading, compared to buying CDs, means no more delivery trucks and no more unnecessary packaging. An iPod, after all, only weighs as much as two boxed CDs, but can hold the same amount of music as 1000.

Isn't copying and downloading music illegal?

No. The only thing that's illegal is taking copyrighted material that you haven't acquired legitimately – and, of course, distributing copyrighted material that you have acquired legitimately. In short, you're well within your rights to copy your own music collection onto your computer and iPod, as long as you don't then copy the files onto your friends' computers or iPods. As for music on the Internet, there are numerous legal options, including online services that sell individual tracks to download and keep, and others which offer unlimited access to a music archive in return for a monthly fee. There's also plenty of downloadable music that's both legal and free: one-off promotions from major labels, for example, and songs by little-known musicians more interested in establishing their name than making a profit.

However, it's true that, at present, the majority of music downloaded from the Internet is copyrighted material taken for free from file-sharing networks such as KaZaA. Though you are unlikely to get prosecuted for taking part in this free-for-all, it is definitely illegal. For the full lowdown on downloading, see p.143.

What's DRM?

As we've already seen, there's nothing the record industry fears more – understandably enough – than the uncontrolled distribution of its copyrighted music. It's hard to see how the record companies will ever be able to stop people sharing files that they have copied from their own CDs, even if they succeed in killing off file-sharing networks like KaZaA (see p.157). However, the labels – and online music retailers – do have a strategy for stopping people freely distributing tracks that they've purchased and downloaded from legitimate online music stores. It's called DRM – digital rights management – and it involves embedding special code into music files (or other formats, such as DVDs) to impose certain restrictions on what you can do with them. For example, music downloaded from the iTunes Music Store has embedded

DRM which stops you from making the tracks available on more than a certain number of computers at one time (for details, see p.148). Other online services, meanwhile, use DRM to stop you burning downloaded files to CD.

Is that an infringement of my rights?

This is a hotly debated issue. Advocates of the free distribution of music see DRM as an infringement of their rights, while others see it as a legitimate way for record labels and retailers to safeguard their products from piracy. So Apple's adoption of the technology has elicited a mixed response. But the DRM debate is really just one part of a bigger argument about whether it's ethical to "share" copyrighted music – and other so-called intellectual

As this spoof poster (available from www.modernhumorist.com) shows, many on the "free distribution" side of the DRM debate see their adversaries – led by the Recording Industry Association of America – as draconian authoritarians committed only to profit, power and an outmoded and unsustainable business model. Unsurprisingly, many musicians disagree.

property. The sharers claim that music is about art not money; that most of the artists whose tracks are being downloaded are already millionaires; that sharing is a great way to experience new music (some of which you might then buy on CD); and that if the record industry really is in trouble, they deserve it for ripping off consumers with overpriced albums for so many years. The industry, on the other hand, says that sharing – or theft, as they prefer to put it – deprives artists of royalties and record labels of the money they need to invest in future albums. The result, they claim, will be fewer musicians and less new music.

It's a complex debate that stretches from the very concept of intellectual property, via different views on the effect of downloading on CD sales, to completely new proposed models for reimbursing musicians, such as the Internet-based "music tax" advocated by some US academics. For both sides of the argument, see:

RIAA www.riaa.com
Electronic Frontier Foundation www.eff.org
The Register www.theregister.com/internet/rights

What about all my CDs?

Unless you're a sound-quality connoisseur or a fan of sleeve notes, you might find that once your music collection has been copied onto your computer and iPod, the original CDs start to seem like a waste of space. Some have advocated selling them: after all, many CDs will go for $10/£5 through online auctions such as eBay, so if you sell enough you can end up far better off than before you bought your iPod. Strictly speaking, though, this is legally dodgy: the moment you sell the CD you are no longer the rightful owner of the music, and technically you should remove it from your computer and Pod.

Getting technical

How is the music stored?

Clever though computers are, they only deal with numbers: digital, rather than analogue, information. In fact, their vocabulary is limited to just zeros and ones: the "binary" number system. So music on a computer or iPod – whether it's a folk song or a symphony – is reduced to a series of millions of zeros or ones. Or, more accurately, it's reduced to a series of tiny magnetic or electronic charges, each representing a zero or a one. A typical song would consist of around 30 million zeros and ones, while a 60GB hard drive in an iPod or computer can hold around 450 billion zeros and ones – roughly 75 for every person on the planet.

But aren't CDs also "digital"?

Absolutely. The idea of reducing music to zeros and ones is nothing new: CDs, MiniDiscs and any other "digital" formats also store music as zeros and ones. But none of these other formats combines the capacity, flexibility and editability of an iPod.

I've heard of MP3s. But what are they exactly?

Computers store information – such as documents, spreadsheets and images – as "files", and there are various different formats for each kind of file. A fancy text document created in Microsoft Word, for example, is saved in the "doc" format, while a simpler text-only document with no fancy styling is usually saved as a "txt" file. Likewise, a professional-quality photo might be in the tif format, while the same image displayed on a website would

19

basics & buying

probably be a JPEG, which looks very nearly as good but is incomparably quicker to download. The format is usually included in a file's name – Memo.doc or John.jpg, for example.

Music on computers (and iPods) can be stored in numerous file formats, but the main ones you need to know about are the ubiquitous MP3 (or Moving Pictures Experts Group-1/2 Audio Layer 3 to give it its rather grandiose full title) and the more recent AAC (Advanced Audio Coding). Like JPEGs for images, these are formats designed for squeezing lots of information into very small files; in fact, technically speaking, the names MP3 and AAC refer not just to the file format but also to the "compression algorithms" used to do the squeezing. Each format has its pros and cons (see p.113), but they both achieve pretty amazing feats of compression. When a computer turns the uncompressed audio information on a CD into MP3 or AAC, the resulting file sounds almost identical to the original but is around ninety percent smaller. That means ten times as much music on your iPod and ten times quicker downloads from the Internet.

This compression is achieved through a remarkable combination of mathematics and psychoacoustics: the algorithms are clever enough to take out what your brain does not process (the vast majority of the sound) and leave the rest untouched. For a full explanation, see: www.mp3-converter.com/mp3codec

Amazing. But my vinyl-junkie friends tell me that CDs are also compressed. Is that true?

Technically speaking, yes, any digital recording could be described as being compressed, since taking the infinitely rich and varied analogue sounds of the real world and turning them into a finite series of numbers inevitably involves losing something. Indeed, many people prefer vinyl (which isn't digital) to CDs for just this reason: they claim it sounds richer and more real. But that's a separate discussion. The point here is that, in the context of iPods, MP3s and the like, "compression" refers to the compressing of digital files into smaller digital files, not the compression of the musicians into numbers.

Each individual track can be compressed to a greater or lesser extent. This is measured in bitrates.

What's a bitrate?

The bitrate of a digital music file is the amount of data (the number of "bits", or zeros and ones) that is used to encode each second of music. This is measured in Kbps: kilo (thousand) bits per second. (Incidentally, if you've ever heard of a "56k modem", the k in that context is short for Kbps and means exactly the same thing: the number of bits transferred per second.) Most music online, on computers and in iPods, is encoded at a bitrate of 128, 160 or 192Kbps, which means that each second of sound is made up of around 100,000 to 200,000 zeros and ones. However, higher and lower bitrates are not uncommon, the latter often being used for spoken-word recordings, where the sound quality is not quite so important.

How big is a gig?

The storage capacity of iPods, like other hard drives, is measured in gigabytes – also called gigs or GBs. Roughly speaking, a byte is eight zeros and ones (the space required on a computer disk to store a single character of text), and a gigabyte is one billion bytes. Or, to compare to other file sizes that you may have come across, a gig is the same as 1000MB (megabytes), which is also the same as 1,000,000KB (kilobytes). Mathematically minded readers may be interested to know that all these figures are actually approximations of the number two raised to different powers. A gigabyte is two bytes to the power of thirty, which equals 1,073,741,824 bytes.

And finally...

Anything else I should know?

In brief, a few common confounders expounded:

▶ **You can't copy music from an iPod to a computer** At least not without extra software (see p.222). The standard setup is that your iPod simply mirrors the Library on your computer.

▶ **You can't delete music from an iPod directly** You have to do it via iTunes. See p.55.

▶ **Playlists are *not* folders containing music files** A playlist (see p.69) is simply a list of songs – adding a song to more than one playlist doesn't duplicate the file, and deleting a playlist doesn't delete the songs in it. See p.71.

▶ **You don't need a playlist for each album** As long as the tracks are tagged, you can view albums in Browse mode. See p.52.

▶ **You don't need to type in CD track names manually** Almost invariably, someone has already done it for you. See p.46.

▶ **Be gentle when pulling a cable from the botton of an iPod** It's held in place with difficult-to-see catches that should be depressed before pulling.

02

Buying an iPod

which model? where from?

There have been various iPod models over the years, but at the time of going to press there are only three types in production: the iPod, the iPod nano, and the iPod shuffle…

▶ **iPod (video model)** The current full-size iPod has been around since October 2005 and is also known as the "fifth generation iPod" or, more widely, the "video iPod", as this was the first model that could handle movie files (see p.179) as well as music and photos. Besides the video function, its primary attractions are its massive storage capacity (see p27 for details), its large, crisp screen, and its ability to connect to a TV to display photos (this requires an extra cable).

basics & buying

▶ **iPod nano** Introduced in September 2005 to replace the colourful iPod mini, the nano is very much like the standard colour-screen iPod, except that the nano is much smaller – both physically and in terms of its storage capacity. Like the iPod shuffle (see below), it stores data on internal flash memory rather than a hard drive, which makes it less prone to skipping and likely to prove more durable. On the other hand, it can't handle videos or connect to a TV to display photos.

▶ **iPod shuffle** The smallest and least expensive member of the iPod family is eminently portable, but it lacks a screen and doesn't allow any browsing of the music stored on it. At any one time, it can store just one playlist – of up to around 125 or 250 songs, depending on the model. Despite popular confusion, you can play through the playlist not only randomly (hence the "shuffle" in its title) but also in fixed order. Like a key drive, it plugs directly into a USB port, as opposed to via a cable.

Phone as iPod

An alternative to a regular iPod is an iTunes-compatible phone, the first of which was released in September 2005. Like a regular iPod, the Motorola ROKR connects to your computer and downloads tracks from your iTunes Library, and it features a Pod-style interface for browsing and playing music. The only problem is that the current model is limited to storing around 100 tracks. The phone is available on the Cingular network in the US, and O$_2$ and T-mobile in the UK. For more information, see www.apple.com/itunes/mobile

iTunes for your mobile phone.

Now Playing

9 of 12

The Journey
Fatboy Slim
Palookaville

-0:59

MENU

MENU

Lifesize Pods: iPod shuffle iPod nano iPod

basics & buying

iPod models: essential specs

Following are the details about the various iPod models available at the time of writing (June 2006). Note that each capacity figure assumes the Pod is

	IPOD SHUFFLE 512MB	IPOD SHUFFLE 1GB	IPOD NANO 1GB
SONG CAPACITY AT...			
128 Kbps (high-quality)	120	240	240
160 Kbps (v-high quality)	100	200	200
192 Kbps (audiophile)	80	160	160
SPOKEN WORD CAPACITY			
Hours at 32 Kbps	35	70	70
PHOTO & VIDEO			
Number of images	n/a	n/a	15,000
Hours of video	n/a	n/a	n/a
SIZE/WEIGHT			
Body (inches)	3.3 x 1 x 0.33	3.3 x 1 x 0.33	3.5 x 1.6 x 0.3
Body (mm)	84 x 25 x 8.4	84 x 25 x 8.4	90 x 40 x 6.9
Weight (ounces)	0.78	0.78	1.5
Weight (grams)	22	22	42
SCREEN			
Diagonal size (inches)	n/a	n/a	1.5
BATTERY			
Maximum life (hours)	12	12	14

being used entirely for music, spoken word, photos or video. For the latest prices and specs, see: www.apple.com/ipod

IPOD NANO 2GB	IPOD NANO 4GB	IPOD 30GB	IPOD 60GB
500	1000	7500	15,000
400	800	6000	12,000
325	650	5000	10,000
135	270	2000	4000
25,000	25,000	25,000	25,000
n/a	n/a	75	150
3.5 x 1.6 x 0.3	3.5 x 1.6 x 0.3	4.1 x 2.4 x 0.33	4.1 x 2.4 x 0.55
90 x 40 x 6.9	90 x 40 x 6.9	104 x 61 x 11	104 x 61 x 14
1.5	1.5	4.8	5.5
42	42	136	157
1.5	1.5	2.5	2.5
14	14	14	20

How many gigs?

Choosing between the various iPod models is above all a matter of choosing how much storage capacity to go for. Remember that you don't necessarily need an iPod capable of holding your whole music collection – or even the collection you intend to digitize. You can store your whole collection on your computer's hard drive and just copy across to your iPod the songs or albums you want to listen to at any one time. That, of course, relies on you having enough space on your computer's hard drive (to find out how to check, see p.11).

One thing worth bearing in mind when it comes to storage capacity is that if you plan to use the iPod as a portable hard drive (see p.167) as well as a digital music player, you'll need enough extra space available for the kinds of files you're planning on storing. Word and Excel docs and the like are almost negligibly small, but backing up your whole system or storing image, video or program files quickly fills up space. Also, note that the "actual" formatted capacity of an iPod (like all hard drives) is more than five percent smaller than advertised. So a 30GB model is really around 28 gigs, and a 4GB model around 3.75 gigs.

Where to buy

As with all Apple products, they cost basically the same amount no matter where you buy them. The price you'll get direct from Apple…

Apple Store UK www.apple.com/ukstore ▶ 0800-039-1010
Apple Store US www.apple.com/store ▶ 1-800-MY-APPLE

…will typically be only a few pounds/dollars more (or occasionally less) than the price you'll find from the many other dealers that sell online or on the high street. That said, different sellers may throw in different extras, from engraving on the back of the iPod to a pair of portable speakers. In the US market you can keep track of these various offers and discounts at the brilliant "Buyers' Guides" section of:

Mac Review Zone www.macreviewzone.com

Or try a price-comparison agent such as, in the US:

Froogle www.froogle.com
PriceWatch www.pricewatch.com
Shopper.com www.shopper.com
Shopping.com www.shopping.com

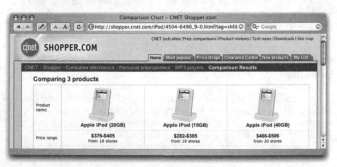

In the UK, price-comparison agents include:

Kelkoo www.kelkoo.co.uk
Shopping.com uk.shopping.com

Buying from a "real" high-street store typically means paying the full standard price, but you'll get the iPod immediately. If you order over the phone or Internet from Apple, you can expect up to a week's wait for delivery. For a list of dealers in the UK, follow the link from www.apple.com/uk/hardware. In London and various US cities, you can go straight to one of Apple's own high-street stores. For a list, see:

Apple Stores www.apple.com/retail

That said, some online retailers tend to be much quicker, including the best known of all:

Amazon US www.amazon.com
Amazon UK www.amazon.co.uk

Laser engraving

If you purchase from Apple, you'll be offered the chance to have a name, slogan or whatever typographic message you like laser-engraved on the iPod's shiny backside. This is the iPod equivalent of a tattoo, so think very carefully as you're stuck with it. If you want a few ideas, to create a virtual engraving to see what it would look like, or just to laugh at some of the best and worst engravings ever requested, visit:

iPod Laughs www.ipodlaughs.com/ipod/iengraver
Methodshop www.methodshop.com/mp3/articles/iPodEngraving

Security-conscious Pod buyers could consider getting their name and either an email address or telephone number engraved on their new gadget. This will give it at least a fighting chance of finding its way back to you if lost; and, if stolen, the thief will have a hard time selling it on.

Used iPods

Refurbished iPods

Apple, and a few retailers, offer refurbished iPods. These are either end-of-line models or up-to-date ones which have been returned for some reason. They come "as new" – checked, repackaged and with a full standard warranty – but they are reduced in price by up to 40 percent (usually more like 15 percent). The only problem is availability: the products are in such hot demand that, in the UK, you can only see Apple's selection on Wednesdays, from 10am onwards (get there early).

Apple Store UK Refurbished
promo.euro.apple.com/promo/refurb/uk

In the US, supply is also limited, though you can at least check whether anything is on offer throughout the week. Follow the Special Deals link from the Apple Store website (www.apple.com/store) or, for the most up-to-date information about availability, call 1-800-MY-APPLE. Alternatively, check with your local Apple retailer to see whether they offer refurbished or returned iPods.

Secondhand iPods

Buying a secondhand iPod is much like buying any other piece of used electronic equipment: you might find a bargain but you might land yourself with an overpriced bookend. That said, the

31

basics & buying

standard Apple warranty is international and, in practice at least, transferable, so if you buy one that is less than a year old (and with the documentation to prove it) you should be able to get it repaired for free if anything goes wrong inside. Obviously, that will rely on the type of damage being covered by the warranty.

Whatever you buy, make sure you see it in action before parting with any cash, but remember that this won't tell you everything. If an iPod's been used a lot, for example, the battery might be on its last legs and soon need replacing, which will add substantially to the cost (see p.240). Also remember that older models won't necessarily support more recent accessories or software.

To buy or to wait?

When shopping for any piece of computer equipment, there's always the tricky question of whether to buy the current model, which may have been around for a few months, or hang on for the next version, which may be better *and* less expensive. In the case of iPods, the situation is worse than normal, because Apple are famously secretive about their plans to release new or upgraded versions of their hardware.

Unless you have a friend who works in Apple HQ – and an opportunity to get them drunk – you're unlikely to hear anything from the horse's mouth about new iPod models until the day they appear. So, unless a new model came out recently, there's always the possibility that your new purchase will be out of date within a few weeks. About the best you can do is check out some sites where rumours of new models are discussed. But don't believe everything you read…

Apple Insider www.appleinsider.com
Mac Rumors www.macrumors.com
Think Secret www.thinksecret.com

Using iTunes & the iPod

03

Getting started

installing, charging, naming

Setting up iTunes and an iPod on your computer isn't difficult, so we won't waste your time here with a step-by-step guide. However, you will be asked a few potentially confusing questions, and there are a few other things worthy of discussion – such as charging your iPod and the all-important question of giving it a name…

Cables and docks

With the exception of iPod shuffles, which plug directly into USB ports, each new Pod comes with a USB2 cable, which will connect to your computer and, if you have one, an AC power adapter. Back in the day, iPods came with FireWire cables, but these have gradually been phased out, and the current iPods and iPod nanos can only talk to iTunes via USB2.

> **TIP:** If your iPod came with both a FireWire and a USB2 cable, consider using one at home and keeping the other in your bag or briefcase. This can be a lifesaver if you unexpectedly want to use your iPod as a hard drive (see p.167).

If, when purchasing the Pod, you also bought a Dock, this little stand will provide a secure spot for your iPod and make it easy for you to connect to both a computer and a hi-fi (see p.208). The Dock simply sits "between" the iPod and the USB2 cable – its use is entirely optional. That said, the Dock provides the only way to connect a colour-screen iPod to a TV via S-Video cable, as opposed to an AV cable, which will plug directly into the Pod (see p.178).

The flat connector slots into your iPod or Dock. When disconnecting, be sure to press the (nearly invisible) release buttons on the sides of the connector

iPod charging

With current iPod models, the standard recharging technique is simply to connect the Pod to your computer. In the vast majority of cases this works fine, though bear in mind that your Mac or PC may need to be on – not in sleep/standby mode. Also note that when a full-size iPod is plugged into your computer, its hard drive will stay active, which some users see as unnecessary wear and tear. If this thought bothers you, consider "ejecting" the Pod (see p.65); this puts it into charge-only mode and puts the drive in stand-by mode.

Like many similar devices, iPods use a combination of "fast" and "trickle" charging. This means that, with a full-size Pod, it should take around two hours to achieve an 80% charge, and another two hours to get to 100%. A new, fully charged iPod should provide between twelve and twenty hours of music playback (see p.26), though just leaving the device lying around and not playing will cause the power level to drain gradually. As the battery ages, expect the maximum playback time to reduce. For tips on maximizing your battery life, see p.240.

If you are unable to charge your Pod via your computer, or you want to be able to charge when away from home, consider buying a separate power adapter. Available from Apple, these cost $29/£19 – much to the annoyance of many iPod owners, as they shipped as standard with earlier models.

Installing…

The process of installing iTunes and an iPod on your computer varies slightly between PC and Mac, and between different iPod models – but it usually simply involves inserting the CD provided with the Pod and following the prompts. At some stage, however, you will be invited to choose a name for your new Pod, which is no laughing matter (see box overleaf). And – either during the installation or the first time you run iTunes – you'll find yourself presented with a few choices. You don't need to worry too much about these as you're just choosing options that can be changed at any time in the iTunes Preferences panel (see p.45). But it's worth understanding what you're being asked…

▶ **Yes, use iTunes for Internet audio content** or
▶ **No, do not alter my Internet settings**
This is asking whether you'd like your computer to use iTunes (as opposed to whatever plug-ins you are currently using) as the program to handle sound and files such as MP3s when surfing the Web. iTunes can do a pretty good job of dealing with online audio, but if you'd rather stick with your existing Internet audio setup, hit No.

▶ **Yes, automatically connect to the Internet** or
▶ **No, ask me before connecting**
iTunes will sometimes want to access the Internet (for example, to find track names for you or access the iTunes Music Store). If you use a standard dial-up Internet connection you probably should select No – this way you won't accidentally block your phoneline or spend extra money (if you pay per minute for access). You can always go online before downloading track names (see p.46) or accessing the iTunes Music Store (see p.143). If you have broadband, however, it's much more convenient to click Yes.

▶ **Do you want to search for music files on your computer and copy them to the iTunes Library?**
Unless you have music files scattered around your computer, and you'd like them automatically put in one place, select No, otherwise you might end up with non-music sound files in your music library. You can always add music – automatically or manually – later (see p.52).

▶ **Do you want to go straight to the iTunes Music Store?**
Decline the invitation for now. For information about downloading from the Apple Music Store and elsewhere, see p.143.

using iTunes & the iPod

The name game

Judging by the number of online chat forums devoted to the subject, naming an iPod is a serious business. The obvious move is to call it "John's Pod", "Jane's Pod", or whatever, but we think you can do better than that. Here are a few weird and wonderful ideas plucked from the World Wide Web:

"I was thinking and thinking of a name for my mini … I looked up Greek and Latin roots and named it 'Parfichlorolocuphone', which means small, green, sound speaker…"

GreenerMini

"doPi (ipod backward) the music elf, as in harry potter rip off of dobby the house elf…"

tombo_jombo

"My iPod's name is 'Glitch', because I had to set it up with Win98SE…"

jesspark

For more inspiration, search Google Groups (www.google.com/groups), or search "Does your iPod have a name" in the forums section of ilounge (www.ilounge.com/forums). If you've already named your iPod, it's not too late to change it: just double-click its name in the iTunes Source List and type something else. But be sure to bear in mind this essential advice…

"Its not bad to change the iPod's name as long as you sit down with it and have a long conversation about what it thinks is best for it."

Kurt8374

39

Once everything's up and running you'll be presented with the iTunes environment – which is the subject of the next section of this book. For more on using your iPod, see p.56.

Get the latest versions

Before getting too comfortable with all the ins and outs of your copy of iTunes, go online and make sure you're running the latest versions of iTunes and iPod Updater. You may be prompted to do this automatically, but you can also do it manually at any time. On a Mac, click "Software Update" from the Apple menu; if a new version of iTunes (or the iPod Updater software) is available, it will appear in the list. On a PC, open iTunes and select "Check For iTunes Updates" from the Help menu.

iTunes
basics

importing, browsing and deleting music

Before diving into advanced functions and settings, file formats, software add-ons, iPod accessories and the rest, let's take a quick spin around iTunes, get everything up and running, rip a few tunes from a CD onto your computer, and get them onto your iPod. Even if you've been using a Pod for years, it's probably worth browsing through this section, as even some of the basic iTunes functions are easy enough to miss – and we've included plenty of tips and tricks.

The iTunes environment

The iTunes application doubles as both a media player for your computer and an interface for your iPod, and some of the controls and buttons will differ depending on whether your Pod is connected. But, in its virgin state, the iTunes environment consists of the following:

Along the top…

Below the application's main menus are, starting from the left, the primary play controls and volume slider, which works independently of your computer's master volume control. Then, in the middle, there's the "status" area, which displays info about the track currently playing or importing and, when you click the small triangular icon on its left, becomes an attractive but fairly worthless EQ display.

Next up is the Search field: type into it to find tracks in your iTunes Music Library. The dropdown menu next to the magnifying-glass icon allows you to choose exactly how you want to search – by artist, album, song, etc.

Finally, there's the circular button on the right, which, again, alters its function depending on what you are doing. When viewing your Music Library it toggles the "Browse" function on and off (see p.53); when a CD is present it prompts you to Import the tracks (see p.46); and when a playlist is selected it gives you the option to burn a CD from that playlist (see p.95).

The Source List

Situated on the left, the Source List is the doorway to your music collection (via the Library icon and playlists), videos (see p.179), Podcasts (see p.163), Internet radio stations (see p.167), other people's shared music (see p.157) and the iTunes Music Store (see p.143). The list also features any CDs or iPod currently attached.

The Song List

The big striped panel that accounts for the majority of the iTunes window lists the songs within whichever source is selected in the Source List. The tracks displayed can be sorted alphabetically or numerically according to any of the various columns of information – click on the top of a column to sort by it. Though the Song List seems at first to be an element of iTunes that needs little elaboration, there are various ways to customize it, the simplest example being the fact that you can adjust the relative size of the two panels by clicking and dragging between the thin silver-grey strip between them. For more on customizing the iTunes Song List, see p.90.

	Name	Artist	Time	Album
1	Sinfonia 10 in G major BWV 796	Glenn Gould	0:57	Bach: Inventions and Sinfonias
2	Sonata 28 in A major, Op 101: IV. ...	Maurizio Pollini	7:33	Beethoven: The Late Piano Sonatas (Disc 1)
3	Six Little Piano Pieces, Op. 19: V. E...	Maurizio Pollini	0:35	Schoenberg & Webern Piano Music
4	No. 13 In F# Major. Prelude	Glenn Gould	2:17	Bach: Well-Tempered Clavier I (Disc 2)
5	Sonata in B minor, Kk 87	Clara Haskil	4:35	Scarlatti: 11 Sonatas
6	Variation 6 – Allegro ma non tropp...	Piotr Anderszewski	1:56	Beethoven: Diabelli Variations
7	Invention 14 in B-flat major BWV 7...	Glenn Gould	1:37	Bach: Inventions and Sinfonias
8	Piano Sonata No.31: III	Piotr Anderszewski	1:40	Bach, Beethoven and Webern Recital
9	Six Little Piano Pieces, Op. 19: III. S...	Maurizio Pollini	1:01	Schoenberg & Webern Piano Music
10	No. 23 In B Major. Fugue	Glenn Gould	1:36	Bach: Well-Tempered Clavier I (Disc 2)
11	English Suite No. 6: VII. Gavotte II-...	Piotr Anderszewski	2:12	Bach, Beethoven and Webern Recital
12	No. 15 In G Major. Fugue	Glenn Gould	2:22	Bach: Well-Tempered Clavier I (Disc 2)
13	Ballata no. 1 op 23 in sol minore	Arturo Benedetti Michelangeli	9:17	Chopin Recital, Vatican, 1986
14	No. 14 In F# Minor. Fugue	Glenn Gould	3:51	Bach: Well-Tempered Clavier I (Disc 2)
15	Sonata in E flat major, Kk 193	Clara Haskil	4:08	Scarlatti: 11 Sonatas
16	Invention 2 in C minor BWV 773	Glenn Gould	2:54	Bach: Inventions and Sinfonias
17	Andante spianato e grande polacca...	Arturo Benedetti Michelangeli	13:03	Chopin Recital, Vatican, 1986

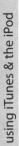

And along the bottom…

To the left there are four buttons. The first adds a new, untitled playlist to the Source List (see p.69 for more on playlists). The second activates the shuffle playback mode (which is also called "random", though you may find it seems distinctly un-random; see p.77). When the third button, with the looping arrows, is clicked and becomes illuminated, whichever source is currently in use (be it a CD, a playlist or your whole Library) will play on cycle ad infinitum. Another click of the same button adds a circled "1" to the icon, which means iTunes will now loop only the individual song. The final button opens a frame at the bottom of the Source List where an image can be placed for that track – the album cover art, for example (see p.93).

On the right there are three more buttons. The first unleashes the iTunes Equalizer window (see p.122), the second turns on the iTunes Visualizer (see p.79), and the third ejects CDs.

Once you start stocking your iTunes Library the lower strip will also start to display useful data in its centre, telling you – for whichever source or playlist that's currently selected – the number of songs present, the total playing time and, most usefully, the total file size the songs collectively take up. This is handy when building playlists to burn to CD, and also offers a means of checking

> **TIP:** You can quickly move between the Source List, the search box and the Song List by pressing the Tab key (with Shift added you move in the opposite order).

exactly how much of your computer's hard drive is being taken up by your collection: to get the bottom line, click the Library icon in the Source List and check the stats.

| + | ✕ | ⟳ | ▽ | 2241 songs, 6.3 days, 8.89 GB | ▮▯▮ | ◉ | ⏏ |

> **TIP:** The total playing time displayed at the bottom of the iTunes window is approximate; click the displayed time and it will change to an exact reading.

iTunes Preferences

iTunes Preferences, which is referred to throughout this book, contains a whole host of options for changing the way iTunes and your iPod work. Preferences can be opened via the iTunes menu (Mac) or the Edit menu (PC). Or you could use the following shortcuts:

Apple+, (Mac)
Ctrl+, (PC)

On Macs,
there's also a
useful shortcut
for moving
between the
various panes:

Next pane:
Apple+]
Previous pane:
Apple+[

General

General iPod Podcasts Playback Sharing Store Advanced Parental

Source Text: Small ⬦   Song Text: Small ⬦

Show: ☑ Party Shuffle
        ☑ Radio

☑ Show genre when browsing
☐ Group compilations when browsing
☐ Show links ◎ to the Music Store

☑ Check for iTunes updates automatically

Cancel   OK

using iTunes & the iPod

Importing music from CD

The best way to get your head around iTunes is to plant some music in it and start playing. Let's start by copying some tracks from a CD to your computer's hard drive. This process is usually known as "ripping"; iTunes, however, calls it "Importing".

You can't really go wrong. Load a CD into your computer and it will appear in iTunes as an icon in the Source List; click the icon and the CD's contents are displayed in the Song List.

Downloading the track names

If, when you originally installed iTunes, you agreed to let it connect to the Internet whenever it feels it needs to, then within a few seconds of loading the CD you'll probably find that the artist, track and album names – and maybe more info besides – automatically appear in the Song List. This information is not pulled from the CD, which contains nothing but music. Rather, it's downloaded via the Internet from CDDB – a giant CD information database hosted by a company called Gracenote (www.gracenote.com).

If iTunes isn't set to connect to the Net automatically, you'll need to tell the program to try and download the track info from CDDB. Connect to the Internet and then select Get CD Track Names from the Advanced menu in iTunes.

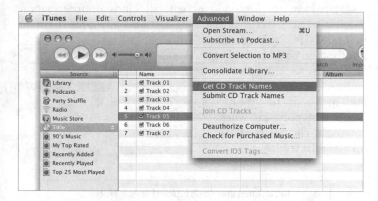

If you get no joy from the CDDB resource, the songs will be left with the titles "Track 1", "Track 2" and so on, and you'll have to input the track info manually (see overleaf). This happens remarkably infrequently, but it's highly likely that the info downloaded may either be inaccurate or won't tally with your own ideas of music categorization – one person's hip-hop is another's R&B, after all. In either case, you'll need to edit the information manually.

> **TIP:** If you rip a few CDs to a laptop when you're out and about and can't get online, you can always access the CDDB database later. Simply select the track or tracks in question (searching for "track" should find them quickly) and click Get CD Track Names from the Advanced menu.

Adding and editing track info manually

You can enter information directly into any editable field of the Song List by clicking on its name twice (not too quickly). Any existing text will become highlighted and you're ready to type. When you're done, click somewhere else in the window or hit Enter.

Alternatively, to view, add or edit all kinds of information about a track, select it in the Song List and hit Apple+I (Mac) or Ctrl+I (PC). The same information box can also be accessed by selecting a track and clicking Get Info in the File menu or the mouse menu that pops up when you right-click (Ctrl+click on a Mac) a track.

	Name	Artist ▲	Time
6	☑ Body And Soul	Billie Holiday	3:26
7	☐ Strange Fruit	iTunes Help	
8	☑ (There Is) No Greater L		
9	☑ Stormy Weather	Get Info	
10	☑ God Bless The Child	Show Song File	
11	☑ Do Nothin' Till You He	My Rating	
12	☑ Don't Explain	Reset Play Count	
13	☑ Fine And Mellow	Convert ID3 Tags...	
14	☑ Life Begins When You'	Convert Selection to AA	
15	☑ It's Like Reaching For		
16	☑ These Foolish Things	Play Next in Party Shuff	
17	☑ I Cried For You		

> **TIP:** If iTunes downloads incorrect or non-existent song info and you have to do some manual entering or editing, select Submit CD Track Names from the iTunes Advanced menu once you're done. Then other people accessing the CDDB service will be able to benefit from your handiwork.

Multiple tracks

To edit or enter information about multiple songs simultaneously, simply select the relevant tracks in the Song List (see box opposite) and press Ctrl+I or Apple+I (or right-click and press Get Info). In the Multiple Song Information box that will pop up, as soon as you make any changes to a field, the box to its left becomes checked. Before you hit OK, make sure only the fields you want to change are checked.

Selecting multiple tracks

To select multiple tracks in the Song List, hold down the Apple key (Mac) or Ctrl key (PC) as you click. Alternatively, to select lots of adjacent tracks at once, click on the first and then Shift+click the last; individual songs can then be removed from this selected group by clicking them while holding down the Apple key (Mac) or the Ctrl key (PC).

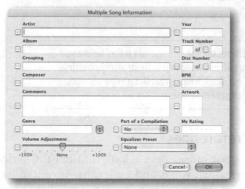

The Multiple Song Information box offers a whole lot more than just basic artist and album details. Tagging, equalizers and volume settings are covered in later chapters

Joining tracks

Before importing the tracks from a CD it's possible to "join" some of them together. Then, when they're played back on your computer or your iPod, they'll always stay together as one unit, and iTunes won't insert a gap between the tracks. This is useful if you have an album in which two or more tracks are segued together (the end of one song merging into the beginning of the next) or if you just think certain tracks should always be heard together (if you joined the three movements of a symphony, for example, the whole work will appear together when you're playing in Shuffle mode).

Simply select the tracks you want to join and then click Join CD Tracks from the Advanced menu. In the short term you can change your mind by clicking Unjoin CD Tracks, but once you've pressed Import, the songs will be imported as a single audio file that cannot be separated without the use of audio-editing software (see p.136).

▲	Song Name
1	☑ ┌ Mara
2	Timo Ma
3	Phaser
4	Danny T
5	Sandra C
6	└ Stef

> **TIP:** iTunes only allows you join tracks before you import. If you want to join them after importing, seek out Track Splicer from Doug's AppleScripts (www.dougscripts.com/itunes).

Import(ant) Preferences

Before importing your music, have a look through the various Importing options, which you'll find under the Advanced pane of iTunes Preferences. The most important settings here are the ones that relate to file formats and sound quality, which are worth considering early on: you don't want to have to re-rip all your CDs a few months down the line if you decide that you're not happy with the sound, or you want to use the tracks with an MP3 player that doesn't support Apple's default AAC format. For more on all of this, turn to p.111.

In the same panel of iTunes Preferences you can also choose how iTunes deals with CDs when they are inserted into your computer. From the On CD Insert dropdown menu you can ask iTunes to automatically start the import process and also eject a CD when it's finished: this is very useful when you are ripping CD after CD, conveyor-belt style.

Importing…

OK, now you've sorted out the track details and file format, it's time to import your CD's songs into the iTunes Library. To the left of each song title in the Song List you'll see a checked tick-box; if you don't wish to import a particular track from a CD, uncheck its box. Now hit the large, round Import button in the upper right-hand corner of the iTunes window and watch as each of your selections is copied to your hard drive.

Where does the music go?

Unless you change the settings, each imported song is saved as an individual file in a hierarchy of folders which reside within your iTunes folder. This can be found within either your Music folder (Mac) or My Documents folder (PC). The hierarchy is defined by the artist and album information of each track. For example, The Beatles' "Dig A Pony" can be tracked down via the following route:

iTunes ▶ iTunes Music ▶ The Beatles ▶ Let It Be ▶ Dig A Pony

As you start to stock your iTunes Library, it becomes important to remain consistent in the way you label your music, or you could end up with multiple entries (and folders) for a single artist. Details retrieved from CDDB are invariably inconsistent (one CD may yield "The Beatles" as the artist, while another might appear labelled "Beatles, The", or simply "Beatles"). Though these kinds of discrepancies don't have any detrimental effect on the way iTunes performs, they can be very annoying when you are browsing for songs on either your computer or your iPod.

Importing from files and folders

As well as getting music into your iTunes library by ripping your CDs or purchasing it from the iTunes Music Store (see p.143), you can also import music files from other locations on your computer or connected storage devices, such as hard drives or flash drives. Simply browse for the files, or folders of files, you want to import and drag them straight into the main iTunes window (or onto a specific playlist icon if you like). The same thing can be achieved by choosing the Add to Library command from the File menu and then pointing to the relevant file or folder.

Note, however, that this will not necessarily copy the actual music files into your iTunes Music folder. Even though you can see the tracks in the iTunes Song List, and use them like any other, the files themselves may still be in their original locations. This is untidy and, furthermore, if the files get moved (for example by a hard drive being unplugged), then iTunes will no longer be able to find the tracks.

To avoid all this, open iTunes Preferences before you start importing and click the Advanced button. Under the General tab make sure that the "Copy files to iTunes Music folder when adding to library" box is checked. Now, after you have imported your songs you can delete the original files from your computer, safe in the knowledge that they have been copied to your iTunes Music folder.

Browsing

Though some people use iTunes for months without noticing it, the "Browse" option is a very important feature, allowing you to browse quickly and easily by genre, artist and album. To open Browse mode, click the eye icon on the toolbar (it may be missing in some circumstances) or select Show Browser from the Edit menu.

> TIP: You'll be using the Browse mode a lot, so for quick access get used to the relevant keyboard shortcuts: Apple+B (Mac) or Ctrl+B (PC).

Browse mode introduces a panel above the Song List, with columns for artist, album and genre. Clicking an entry under Genre reveals the artists from that genre; clicking an entry under Artists, in turn, reveals all the albums of that artist. And, with each selection, the Song List changes to display only the relevant songs.

> **TIP:** You can edit track info from the Browse lists, which
> is handy for quickly changing all "Beatles" tracks, say, to
> "The Beatles". Simply select an artist or album – or even
> a whole genre – and press Apple+I (Mac) or Ctrl+I (PC). This
> is very useful, but proceed with care – you can't undo it if you
> make a mistake.

You'll find a couple of options for Browse mode under the
General pane of iTunes Preferences. Here, you can turn the Genre
column on and off, and also specify whether you want albums that
are tagged as compilations to appear within the Artist column.

Searching

The Search box, on the right-hand side at the
top of the iTunes environment, lets you find a
track by typing all or part of the name of the
artist, album, track title or composer. You can search more than
one field at once, so typing *Bee Vio*, for example, would bring up
Beethoven's Violin Concerto.

If you get too many results, you can limit them using the strip of
buttons that appears just below the status area.

Note that iTunes will only search those tracks currently in the
Song List. So if you want to search your whole collection, make
sure that the Library icon is selected in the Source List, and "All"
is selected in the Genre column before you start to type.

Deleting music from iTunes

There are several ways to delete music from the iTunes Library. But however you do it, first make sure that Library is selected in the Source List and then select the song or songs you want to ditch in the Song List. Deleting files from a playlist (see p.71) does not delete the actual file from the iTunes Library – only the playlist's reference to the file.

If you want to remove a whole album, artist or genre from your collection, open the Browse mode and select the relevant entry in the list. Then, either…

▶ **Hit Backspace or Delete** on your keyboard.

▶ **Select Clear** from the iTunes Edit menu.

▶ **Right-click (PC) or Ctrl+click (Mac)** the items and select Clear from the mouse menu.

▶ **Drag the selections straight to the Trash (Mac only)**

When asked, opt to send the files to the Trash, otherwise they'll remain in your iTunes folder, taking up space unnecessarily.

> ▶ TIP: Deleting music as described above will send the files to your Recycle Bin or Trash, ready to be permanently deleted. If you want to remove something from iTunes but not delete it from your computer, the tidiest way is to right-click the song and select Show Song File to locate the relevant file. Copy this file somewhere safe, then return to iTunes and remove the original.

05

iPod
basics

what you need to know

Using an iPod really is a breeze. And yet there are quite a few options and features – both on the iPod itself and in the way it interacts with iTunes – that pass many users by. So, while some of what follows is self-explanatory, you're sure to learn something…

Adding music to an iPod

In most cases, your iPod will – by default – be set to automatically synchronize itself with the contents of your iTunes Library, making an exact match of all your songs and playlists (see p.69) whenever you connect it to your computer. All you have to do is sit back and wait for a message in the iTunes Status area informing you that the update is complete. The first time you do this it can take a while, but after that it's typically very quick, depending on how many songs you've added or changed in iTunes since your last update.

It's worth noting that this sync will also delete tracks: if there's something on your iPod that's not on your computer, it will be removed when you plug in the Pod. Furthermore, it's a one-way process, reproducing your iTunes Library on your iPod – not the other way around.

> ▶ TIP: If your iPod is set to update automatically and you want to stop this happening (for example, to access iPod Preferences and turn off automatic updating) hold down Apple+Alt (Mac) or Ctrl+Alt (PC) for a few seconds while attaching the iPod.

Other options

If you'd rather not have iTunes automatically update your iPod, you can turn this option off within the iPod Preferences pane (see overleaf). There are two alternatives:

Automatically update selected playlists only

This option is useful if you have an iPod without the capacity to hold your whole collection; you want to save time when updating your iPod; or if you want to leave some space on your Pod

iPod Preferences

To open the iPod Preferences panel, where you can make various changes to how the iPod interacts with your computer, select the iPod icon in the Source List and then click the iPod button that appears at the bottom of iTunes. Alternatively, Ctrl+click (Mac) or right-click (PC) the icon of your Pod in the Source List and press iPod Options…

for non-music files. It's also handy if you're using multiple iPods with a single copy of iTunes – each user can simply organize their preferred tracks into a specific set of playlists. For more on playlists, see p.69.

Manually manage songs and playlists

This gives you complete control over the contents of your iPod. When selected, you update your Pod by dragging tracks, albums, artists, playlists or genres from the iTunes Library onto the iPod icon in the Source List. You can also drag directly into any playlists on the iPod (click the small triangle next to the iPod's icon in the Source List to view them).

In this "manual mode" you can also remove songs or playlists from your iPod: click the Pod's icon; select one or more

> TIP: None of these various sync and manual modes allow you to copy songs from an iPod to iTunes. But this can be done (see p.222).

Filling up an iPod shuffle

Just like other iPod models, the iPod shuffle appears in the Source list and is automatically updated when connected. However, unlike with its screened siblings, when the shuffle is connected to a Mac or PC, iTunes presents you with the "Autofill" panel, which pops up below the Song list. Here, you can choose how (random/non-random) and from where (your whole library or a specific playlist) you want the shuffle to be filled each time you connect. Mess about with the various settings to see what suits you best, or turn the function off altogether and manage your shuffle's contents manually.

With less than a gig of storage capacity, shuffle real estate is obviously at a premium. To help you get as much music loaded as possible, the shuffle will not play space-heavy AIFF or Apple Lossless files, or any files with a bitrate higher than 128Kbps. However, when you enable the feature within the iPod pane in iTunes Preferences, any such songs will be re-sampled to become more space-efficient 128Kbps AAC files, on the fly, while your iPod shuffle is being updated.

If you want to see what's on your iPod shuffle even when it's not connected to your computer, select the "Keep this iPod in the source list" in the iPod pane of iTunes Preferences. This also allows you to try out various Autofill concoctions before you connect and update the shuffle.

items from the Song List; and select Clear from the Edit or right-click menus. It's worth noting, however, that, as in iTunes, removing a song from a playlist only removes it from the playlist – not from the iPod.

Adding music from other computers

By default, if you plug your iPod into someone else's computer, iTunes will offer to completely replace your music Library with theirs (assuming, that is, you're not connecting a Mac-formatted

using iTunes & the iPod

iPod to a PC, in which case it won't work at all: see p.172). If you say yes, next time you connect at home you'll get the same choice – keep the new Library or replace it with your own.

This set up is specifically designed to prevent the unauthorized copying of music. However, it's a real pain if you have more than one computer, or if you want to copy something copyright free from a friend's Mac or PC.

To get around this, you could switch on "Manually manage songs and playlists" (see p.58) and copy across the tracks you want. This will allow you to combine music from more than one computer on your Pod, but it will also lock you in to manually managing your music – the moment you switch back to the automatic mode, everything will be removed from the Pod, only to be replaced by the Library of whichever PC or Mac you're working on.

A better alternative is to enable your iPod as a hard drive (see p.171) and use it to transfer the actual song files to your own (or main) computer, as described on p.106.

Deleting music from an iPod

Many a new iPod user has pulled their hair out trying to delete unwanted music directly from a Pod. The solution is simple: you can't do it on the Pod itself, you have to do it via iTunes. Assuming you have your iPod set to automatically update all songs and play-lists, you have a few options:

▶ **Simply delete music from iTunes (see p.55)** and the next time you connect your iPod, the tracks will disappear from there, too.

▶ **Or, if you want the music on iTunes but not on your iPod,** uncheck the little boxes next to the names of the offending tracks, and in iPod Preferences select "Only update checked songs".

▶ **Or, if don't want to uncheck the songs** (since this will stop them playing in iTunes too), use one of the manual update options described on p.58 to take more control over exactly what gets transferred to your iPod.

The iPod controls

Once your Pod's loaded up with tunes and disconnected from your computer, you're ready to start exploring the various buttons and menus. Again, these are very straightforward, though there are more options than at first meet the eye.

The controls

The iPod controls have altered slightly with each new design, but whichever you have, they're pretty intuitive (though the sensitivity of touch required may lead to gritting of teeth at first). Overleaf is a rundown of what each button does on all click-wheel iPods, where the four buttons are integrated at the four compass points of the scroll wheel. Besides the controls mentioned here, there are also button combinations used for troubleshooting and resetting (see p.236).

Browsing the menus

The iPod's hierarchy of menus and submenus is pretty self-explanatory, and best explored by trial and error, so we won't patronize or bore you with a complete walk-through here. Suffice to say that you browse to a track, album or playlist and

iPod	
Music	>
Photos	>
Videos	>
Extras	>
Settings	>
Shuffle Songs	

61

Hold switch
Get used to using this to disable the other controls – especially when you're not using your iPod.

Select button Use this to make selections in menus, or start playing a highlighted song. When a tune is playing, the button also selects between volume, rating and scrubbing. Held down, it adds tracks to the On-The-Go playlist.

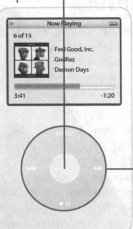

Click wheel
Besides letting you scroll through menus, this wheel alters the volume when you're listening to music. It also features the four main control buttons described below.

Now Playing

6 of 15

Feel Good, Inc.
Gorillaz
Demon Days

3:41   -1:20

MENU As well as taking you back through the menus when clicked, this button turns on the iPod's backlight when held down.

I◀◀ A single click takes you back to the start of a track, a second click and you're back at the start of the previously played track (not necessarily the previous track in the album or playlist); hold down this button and you skip-search back through the currently playing track.

▶II The iPod doesn't have a "stop" button; instead, you simply pause and unpause the music with this button. It also turns the iPod off when held down.

▶▶I Just like the back skip/rewind button, only forwards.

press the Select button to set it going. If you find yourself lost, simply backtrack using the Menu button until you know where you are again.

Here are a few tips and tricks to ease your browsing and help you get the most from your Pod's controls…

▶ **Clicks** By default the iPod clicks repeatedly whenever you touch either the scroll wheel or a button. As well as being a slight waste of battery power, this will win you no friends when travelling on public transport. To disable the clicks, scroll to Settings, then Clicker, and use the Select button to choose Off.

▶ **Customizing** Under Main Menu in Settings, you can choose exactly which browsing categories you want to access from your Pod's top-level menu. Classical buffs, for example, may want to add "Composer".

▶ **Scrubbing** This term means speeding through a song visually, rather than aurally. When a track is playing, hit the Select button once and you should see a little diamond shape representing your

Shuffle and Repeat on the iPod

The main menu on recent iPods contains an option to Shuffle Songs, which picks tracks randomly from your entire Library. If you look within the Settings menu, however, you'll find more advanced options. If you turn on Shuffle here, individual playlists or albums will play back in random order. And you can also opt to Shuffle by albums instead of tracks. The same menu also gives you options for Repeat, but bear in mind that if your iPod is set to play forever, you'll be more likely to run down your battery (or damage your earphones) if you forget to use the Hold switch and the Pod gets turned on accidentally in your pocket.

current position in the song. Move this forwards or backwards using the scroll wheel and then press Select.

▶ **Contrast** If your menus are hard to read, navigate to Contrast, within Settings, and use the scroll wheel to adjust the setting.

▶ **Rating tracks** Pressing the Select button twice will allow you to rate a track (see p.88).

▶ **Now playing** When listening to one track, you can browse through the other tracks and menus as usual – just press Menu and off you go. If you do this, however, you won't be able to use the scroll wheel to either scrub or change the volume and rating until you return to the track you are currently playing. To do this return to the Main Menu and then choose Now Playing (at the bottom of the list).

▶ **Making playlists** When browsing through tracks, holding down the Select button for a couple of seconds will add a highlighted song to the iPod's On-The-Go playlist (see p.66).

▶ **About...** To see how much space you have left on the iPod, click About within the Settings menu. This function can be unreliable,

> TIP: Be careful if exploring the Language settings. If you accidentally choose a language you don't understand, you may struggle to get things back to how they were. If this happens, see p.239 for help.

Disconnecting an iPod

Depending on a few factors, an attached iPod may display the warning "Do not disconnect". If so, you'll need to "unmount" your iPod before unplugging the cable. To do this, either:

 Click the eject icon to the right of the iPod icon in the Source List (see below).

 Click the eject button in the bottom right corner of the iTunes window (see below).

 Ctrl+click (Mac) or right-click (PC) the iPod icon in the Source List and select Eject…

Drag its Desktop icon to the Trash (only on Macs, and with Hard Disk Mode enabled, see p.172).

If you simply disconnect the device without properly dismounting it, you could end up mashing song data, crashing your computer or even damaging the hard drive in your iPod, so get into the habit of doing it properly. And even when following one of the correct procedures, don't physically pull the plug, or remove your Pod from the Dock, until the iPod's screen displays the regular menu. On older Pods a large tick icon appears to inform you that the dismount was successful.

If the iPod refuses to unmount, and the "Do not disconnect" message stays on the screen, there may be a problem. Turn to the Troubleshooting chapter (see p.235).

though, so if you want to be certain, attach your iPod to your computer and look on the bottom of the iTunes windows.

On-The-Go Playlists

If you're out and about and you want to set up a playlist there and then, you can do so with the iPod's On-The-Go Playlist function. Browse your music and when you come across a song, artist, album or even a whole genre that you'd like to add, press and hold the Select button. After around a second the selection's name will flash to let you know that it has been added to the On-The-Go Playlist – which you'll find at the bottom of the Playlists menu. Repeat the process for as many selections as you like.

> TIP: You can add to an On-The-Go Playlist while it's playing. For example, you could add one track, set the Playlist going, and then add more.

You can easily clear or save your On-The-Go Playlist using the options that you'll find within the list itself, below the tracks. When you save such a playlist, it will appear as "New Playlist 1" and be transferred to iTunes next time you connect your Pod to your computer. You can create and save as many On-The-Go Playlists as you want.

Volume Limit

There has been much talk in the press in recent years about the damage we are all doing to our ears by being permanently "wired for sound". Volume Limit, Apple's response to the problem, features on all video iPods and iPod nanos. Found in the Settings menu, this feature is primarily designed to allow parents to stop their kids from using their iPods at extreme, ear-crunching volumes (you can even set a four-digit combination lock so that your pride and joy can't reset the limit when you're not looking). However, it can also be handy for protecting earphones or headphones from damage – especially

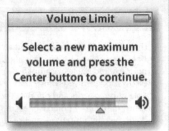

expensive ones, which generally don't need to be "driven" as hard as cheaper pairs.

Screen Lock

Screen Lock (again, found on video iPods and nanos only) lives in the Extras menu. When activated, it will stop people using your iPod to listen to music without your permission. Perhaps more usefully, it will also keep prying eyes away from private data – such as contacts, calendars and notes. Just like the Volume Limit, it works using a four-digit

combination code. If you forget the code, plugging into iTunes will allow you to unlock the Pod.

Crash!

It probably won't be long before your iPod does something strange – such as failing to respond when you press the buttons. In these situations, you'll need to reset your Pod (see p.236) and maybe update your iPod software (see p.40).

using iTunes & the iPod

That's not an iPod...

iTunes is inextricably associated with the iPod, and it's true that the iPod is the only portable device officially supported by the program (the Motorola ROKR phone being one exception). However, though few people realize it, it's possible to shoehorn your music library (and more in some cases) into other portable music players and phones. The only catch is that this won't work with songs that you've purchased from iTunes, which can only be put on another device via time-intensive and/or legally dodgy techniques (see p.156).

When connected, some non-iPod MP3 players and phones may appear in the iTunes Source List, but iTunes won't automatically fill them up with tracks as it would an iPod. Furthermore, to add tracks manually to such a device, you'd have to convert any AAC files into MP3 files (see p.119). Thankfully, there are now various little programs that will make the job much quicker, enabling you to easily get your playlists onto everything from a PSP to a Creative Zen.

▶ **Thrupp** www.utsire.com/thrupp (Mac) $15
An intuitive little application that will let you get music onto any MP3 player or phone that appears as a drive when connected to a Mac.

▶ **BadApple** www.badfruit.com (PC) Free
A handy PC plug-in that works with loads of MP3 player brands, including Creative, Dell and even the Oakley Thump MP3 sunglasses.

▶ **PocketMac for PSP** www.pocketmac.net (OS X) $10
Lets you sync music from iTunes playlists directly onto the PSP's memory cards. At the same time you can sync your PSP with Apple's iPhoto and Address Book.

▶ **PSPWare** www.nullriver.com (OS X) $15
More feature-heavy than PocketMac, PSPWare syncs iTunes music, but also movies and photos while additionally backing up your gaming data.

▶ **iTunes-PSP** www.skattertech.com/2006/04/stream-itunes-library-to-psp (PC) Free
The problem with both PSPWare and PocketMac for PSP is that they are trying to squeeze loads of files into a memory stick that's nowhere near as capacious as most iPods. This alternative solution lets you keep your music on your computer and stream it wirelessly across your home to the PSP.

06 Playlists

the new mix tape

A key feature of any computer jukebox software is the ability to create playlists: homemade combinations of tracks for playing on your computer or iPod; for burning to CD; for sending to friends; or even for publishing online. Like the old-fashioned mix tape, a playlist can be made for a particular time, place or person, or just for fun. Unlike with cassettes, however, playlists can be created instantly; they can be as long as you like; they won't be poor sound quality; and there's no need to buy physical media.

using iTunes & the iPod

The basics

The first thing to understand about playlists is that they don't actually contain any music. All they contain is a list of pointers to tracks within your iTunes Library. This means you can delete playlists, and individual tracks within them, without deleting the actual music files; likewise, you can add the same track to as many playlists as you like without using up extra disk space.

Playlists appear in the Source List (along with the icons for Library, Radio, etc) and they're completely editable at any time. You can drag one or more songs into a playlist from the Song List, or – using Browse mode – you can even drag in an entire artist, genre or album's contents in one fell swoop. Once a playlist is highlighted in the Source List, its contents become available in the Song List, allowing you to play, delete or rearrange the tracks at will. And, next time you update, your playlists will be copied across to your iPod.

iTunes probably came with a few Smart Playlists (more on what this means below) labelled "90's Music", "My Top Rated", etc. Don't be scared to delete them.

Creating playlists

To create a new playlist, either hit the new playlist button (the +) at the bottom of the Source List, or press Apple+N (Mac) or Ctrl+N (PC). Either way, a new playlist icon will appear in the Source List, high-lighted and ready to be named and filled. Try it: create and name a playlist; click on the Library icon to view all your music; and drag some random tracks onto your playlist's icon.

You can also create a new playlist by dragging songs, artists, albums or genres directly into some blank space at the end of the Source List. A new playlist of those cuts will appear and iTunes will even try to name it according to the tracks being dragged (you can always change it manually; see below).

> ▶ TIP: You'll find a "New playlist from selection" option in the Edit menu. Holding Shift and clicking the New Playlist button (Mac) or pressing Ctrl+Shift+N (PC) has the same effect.

Rearranging, renaming and deleting playlists

You can sort the contents of a playlist automatically by clicking the top of the columns in the Song List. Or, to sort them manually, first sort by the number column and then drag the tracks at will.

To rename a playlist, click its name once and then again (not too fast). To delete one, highlight it and press the backspace key; select Clear from the Edit or right-click menus; or, on a Mac, drag the icon into the Trash.

> ▶ TIP: If you want to delete a playlist without being asked to confirm, hold down Apple (Mac) or Ctrl (PC) while you hit backspace. Or, to make this the default option, check "Do not ask me again" in the delete playlist confirmation box.

Smart Playlists

Smart Playlists are just like normal playlists but, rather than being compiled manually by you, iTunes does the work on your behalf, collecting all tracks in your Library that fulfil a set of rules, or "conditions", that you define. It might be songs that have a certain word in their title, or a set of genres, or the tracks you listened to the most – or a combination of any of these kinds of things. The really clever thing about Smart Playlists is that their contents will automatically change over time, as relevant tracks are added to your Library or existing tracks meet the criteria by being, say, rated highly.

To create a new Smart Playlist, look in the File menu or click the New Playlist button while holding down Alt (Mac) or Shift (PC) – you'll see the plus sign change into a cog. This will open the Smart Playlist box (as shown above), where you set the parameters for the new list. Simply click + and – to add and remove rules. It's a bit like a bizarre kind of musical algebra.

> **TIP:** If you have an iPod without enough space to hold your whole music collection, make a Smart Playlist for the tracks you want to upload. You might, for example, exclude all tracks: with a high bitrate; in AIFF, WAV or Apple Lossless format; with a low star rating; and so on. Then check the box for "Limit To", and enter the capacity of your iPod minus around 10 percent, and also check the box for Live Updating. Then in iPod Preferences (see p.58), select "Automatically update selected playlists only", and choose the relevant playlist.

Smart Playlist ideas

Smart Playlists give you the opportunity to be creative with the way you organize the songs in your Library; they can be both a lot of fun and very useful. So much so, in fact, that there are whole websites devoted to the subject (such as www.smartplaylists.com).

Following are a few examples to give you an idea of the kinds of things you can do with Smart Playlist.

Functional...

Tracks I've never heard
▶ Play Count is 0
Lets you hear music that you've ripped or downloaded but not yet played.

On the up
▶ Date Added is in the last 30 days
▶ My Rating is greater than 3 stars
▶ Play Count is less than 5
A playlist of new songs that you like, but which deserve more of a listen.

The old Joanna
▶ Grouping contains piano
If you use Grouping or Comment fields (see p.88) to tag tracks by instrument, mood or anything else, you can then create Smart Playlists based on this info.

...or inspirational

A compilation of questions
▶ Song Name contains "?"
For days with no answers.

Space songs
▶ Song Name contains "space"
▶ Song Name contains "stars"
▶ Song Name contains "moon"
▶ Song Name contains "rocket"
For those who love their sci-fi as much as their music.

To edit the rules of an existing Smart Playlist, select it and choose Edit Smart Playlist in the File menu – or in the menu you get by right-clicking (PC) or Ctrl-clicking (Mac).

Playlist folders

Once you've amassed scores of playlists, you may find it useful to keep them organized in folders. You'll find the option to create a folder within the File menu. Once you've created one, you can simply drag playlists – or even other folders – into it.

At the time of writing, playlist folders aren't supported on iPods – though all the playlists within them are copied over as usual.

And then...

So you've created a dream playlist, and it's just too good to keep all for yourself. What next? You could:

▶ **Burn it to CD** (see p.95)

▶ **Design the artwork** (see p.101)

▶ **Publish it as an iMix** (see p.149)

▶ **Air it at a London nightclub** (see p.252)

You could even send it to us at Rough Guides (using the address playlists@roughguides.com), and we might just publish it in this book's companion volume: *The Rough Guide Book of Playlists*.

07

Playing in iTunes

options and troubleshooting for playback

iTunes provides various tools for use when music is playing, from the obvious – such as a selection of repeat and random modes – to the less obvious, such as a simple means of chopping off the beginning or end of tracks. There are also ways of accessing the iTunes controls without opening the program's main window. Following is the lowdown on each, plus tips on diagnosing what's wrong when a track won't play back.

Play modes

In its default state, iTunes will play whatever is in the Song List, in the order shown in the Song List, and then stop. But there are various other options…

Repeat

Most CD players offer you the option of playing a single track or album on "loop" – round and round until you beg it to stop. And so it is with iTunes: select Repeat All  and whatever is in the Song List (whether it's an album, a playlist, a CD or your whole Library) will play round and round forever. Select Repeat One and only the track currently playing will loop. You can access these options via the Controls menu or with the Repeat button below the Source List.

Shuffle

When the Shuffle option is turned on, iTunes plays back the contents of the Song List in random order – though random isn't necessarily the right word (see box opposite). This function can be toggled on and off by using either the Controls menu or the Shuffle button below the Source List.

> ▶ TIP: If you have Shuffle mode on and you want to see what's coming next, click the top of the track number column in the Song List. If you don't like the order iTunes has selected, reshuffle by turning Shuffle mode off and back on, or by holding down Alt (Mac) or Shift (PC) and clicking the Shuffle button once.

> ▶ TIP: On the iPod, you can choose between the various
> Shuffle and Repeat modes within the Settings menu.
> These give you more control than simply pressing
> Shuffle Songs in the main menu.

Smart shuffle

Though there's no such thing as true random-order generation, computers and their programmers can do an excellent job of simulating genuine disorder. But ever since the early days of iTunes and iPods, users have complained of a distinct presence of pattern, even predictability, in the "random" selections generated by the Shuffle mode. Perhaps it's just superstition – no one outside Apple HQ seems to know how Shuffle actually works – but people claim to hear certain artists or tunes appearing more than others, and genres or artists appearing in chunks rather than evenly spread out.

iTunes 5 improved things with the introduction of Smart Shuffle, which lets you choose from a sliding scale of randomness, from "more likely" (related songs and genres will tend to follow each other) to "less likely" (expect decidedly odd juxtapositions). Furthermore, you can now choose to have your Shuffle mode proceed by whole albums or groupings instead of individual songs. You'll find these options in iTunes Preferences, under Playback.

If you want to add to your long-term randomness, try ensuring that Shuffle mode doesn't return to one track until it has played all the others, even between multiple listening sessions. To do this, create a Smart Playlist (see p.71) for songs which have a Play Count of less than, say, two. When the music finally stops, change the Play Count setting to 3. And so on...

One final Shuffle tip: if you don't want a specific track to appear in any Shuffle selections, highlight the track, press Get Info in the File menu and, under Options, select "Skip when shuffling".

using iTunes & the iPod

Party Shuffle

Party Shuffle, found in the Source List, is a play mode that generates a random mix of tracks drawn from either a playlist of your choice or your entire Library. When Party Shuffle is being used, a new

panel appears at the bottom of the Song List, in which you can set parameters for how the list looks and where the tracks are drawn from, though you can also add selections from anywhere in your Library by dragging them onto the Party Shuffle icon in the Source List. At any time you can regenerate the track list either manually – by dragging them up and down – or automatically, by hitting the Refresh button in the top right corner of the iTunes window (this will replace the list's contents with fresh selections, but not remove manually added songs).

If you don't want to see the Party Shuffle icon in the Source List, you can choose to hide it by unchecking the box under the General settings in iTunes Preferences.

Visualizer

If you are not content just to sit and watch a small dot plodding its way across the iTunes status area as your songs play, then turn on the iTunes Visualizer: a psychedelic light show that swirls and morphs in time with the music. Depending on your taste, it will either hypnotize you into a state of blissful paralysis or – more likely – annoy the hell out of you.

The Visualizer can be turned on or off by clicking its button in the bottom right corner of the iTunes window (the one with the little flower-like icon). There's also a Visualizer menu where you can set how large you want the visuals to appear in the iTunes window and enable or disable the full-screen mode, with which the swirling patterns take over your whole monitor, just like a screen saver.

When the Visualizer is doing its thing, the button in the top right corner of the iTunes window can be used to open the Options

using iTunes & the iPod

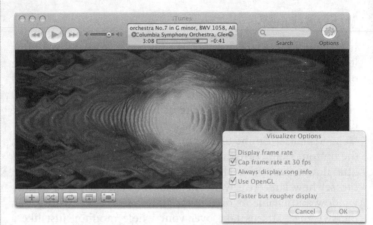

pane. Some of the choices are self-explanatory, but others are less so. Unchecking the "Cap frame rate" box may allow you to improve the visuals, but will add an extra burden onto your system resources (which might, for example, slow down other applications). And "Use OpenGL" should be left checked unless you have reason to turn it off (see box below).

OpenGL

OpenGL is a global standard for 3D (and 2D) computer graphics development. The idea is that with this standard in place both hardware and software developers can be sure that new machines will support applications that rely on advanced graphics, and new software that features advanced graphics will run smoothly on any machine with any operating system. However, you may find that some Visualizer plug-ins (see p.82) don't work with your iTunes setup – if this is the case, try disabling OpenGL in the Options pane. For more see:

OpenGL.org www.opengl.org

Visualizer shortcuts

You can also use a number of keyboard shortcuts to adjust the settings while the Visualizer is playing.

▶ **Z & X** Varies the current colour scheme.

▶ **A & S** Cycles through the waveforms of the current pattern.

▶ **Q & W** Cycles through the various patterns.

▶ **R** Randomly selects a new style and colour.

▶ **C** Displays information about the current pattern (they all have fitting names, such as "diamond tiled tunnel").

▶ **M** Toggles between play modes. In "Random slideshow" mode, iTunes picks the patterns arbitrarily; in "User config slideshow", iTunes picks from your presets (see the Tip box below); in "Freezing current" mode, a single pattern continues indefinitely.

▶ **I** Displays info and cover art for currently playing track.

▶ **D** Return to default settings.

▶ **B** Places the Apple logo in the centre of the Visualizer screen (just in case you forget who you have to thank for all the patterns).

▶ **F** Displays the frame rate.

▶ **T** Turns frame-rate cap on/off.

> **TIP:** If you see a pattern you like, hold down Shift and a number key (0–9). Then you can recall the pattern at any time by pressing the relevant key. And if you turn on "User config slideshow" with the M key, iTunes will combine your preset choices.

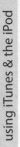

Visualizer plug-ins

If you get bored of the built-in iTunes visuals you can always add more. There are loads to be found online, at sites such as:

Arkaos www.arkaos.net
JCode www.jcode.org
PluginsWorld.com www.pluginsworld.com

Once you've downloaded some plug-ins, they're very easy to install. On a Mac, drag them to the iTunes Plug-ins folder (which can be found within iTunes, within Library, within your Home folder); or, if you have multiple users set up on your computer and you want the plug-in to be available to all, drag them to the iTunes Plug-ins folder located in the iTunes folder in the main Library folder of your Macintosh HD (if the iTunes Plug-ins folder isn't there, create it). On a PC, the iTunes Plug-ins folder can be found in the iTunes folder within the My Music folder. Again, if there isn't one there, create a new folder.

Minimizing and miniaturizing

As with any other program, iTunes windows can be resized by dragging the bottom right corner, and also minimized – hidden from view but still active and accessible via the Dock (on a Mac) or Taskbar (in PC). This is done in the normal way: on a Mac, click the small yellow button in the top left corner of the window, or press Apple+M; on a PC, click the minimize button on the window's top right corner, or press M while holding down the Windows key.

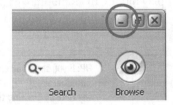

This is all standard stuff but, unlike most other programs, iTunes also provides a halfway house between a window being open and minimized: a miniaturized

version offering access to essential player controls and, if desired, the status display. This is great if you want to keep an eye on what's playing, skip tracks you don't like and so on, while working in another program. To transform iTunes into a miniaturized player, click the small green button in the top left of the window (Mac) or press Ctrl+M (PC). The mini player that pops up can be further shrunk by dragging its corner.

> TIP: On a Mac you can also access a menu of the most useful iTunes controls by clicking and holding the mouse over the iTunes icon on the OS X Dock. The PC version offers something similar via the iTunes icon in the System Tray (by the clock).

✓ ☐ iTunes

✓ Repeat Off
Repeat All
Repeat One

✓ Shuffle

Play
Next Song
Previous Song

Show In Finder
Hide
Quit

Start/stop times

If you've long been bugged by something at the beginning or end of a track – an extended fade, a concert recording applause, a snippet of indulgent band banter, or whatever – now is your chance to excise it. Whether you've ripped the track from CD or downloaded it, it can be topped and tailed in iTunes. Let's take, for example, The Beatles' "Good Morning, Good Morning", which opens with the crow of a cockerel. If you listened to the song and kept an eye on the iTunes status area, you'd see that the cockerel's moment of glory lasts a good two seconds, and the band don't start playing until the display reads "Elapsed time: 0.03".

To erase the offending bird, we first need to select the track in the Song List and select Get Info from the File menu. Under the Options panel in the box that pops up, there are boxes for the song's current Start Time (which, as you might expect, is 0:00) and Stop Time. Now we can simply highlight the start time and type a new value – in this example, 0:03 seconds. Then we can click OK and listen back to the song to see if the new setting is accurate enough. If not, we can go back into the Options pane and tweak the time – entering fractions of a second after a colon, if necessary (eg, 0:03:50).

Trimming the end works in just the same way. And whichever end you're changing, you're not harming the song file, only the way iTunes plays it, so none of this is permanent. If you felt bad about the cockerel, say, you could simply return to the Options panel and reinstate him.

> TIP: For more serious editing of tracks – from trimming them to combining them – you'll need to use a wave-editing program. See p.136.

Problems playing songs

There are several reasons why a song might not play, but in most cases iTunes will inform you what the problem is. If it fails to offer an explanation, however, check the following:

▶ **Is the volume turned up?** Check that both the iTunes volume slider and your computer's master volume are turned up.

▶ **Are you authorized?** If you have exceeded the number of PCs or Macs on which you are allowed to play tracks purchased from iTunes (see p.148) they won't play until you deauthorize one machine and authorize the one you are trying to use (see p.149).

▶ **Is it an iTunes AAC file?** Though a track that you've found online may appear to be an AAC file (see p.113), if it wasn't created in iTunes or purchased from the iTunes Music Store (see p.143) you may not be able to play it.

▶ **Is your Internet connection too slow?** If you are having problems playing streaming previews from the iTunes Music Store, you might find it better to download the entire preview before hearing it. Open iTunes Preferences, and under Store check the "Load complete preview before playing" box.

▶ **Does your playlist contain previews?** Playlists that contain previews (see p.147) copied from the iTunes Music Store will halt the playback of a playlist after each preview; you'll need to double-click the next song in the playlist to hear it.

A few final tips for playback…

▶ **When a song is playing but you've browsed elsewhere**, use the SnapBack arrow in the right of the status area to show the currently playing song in the Song List.

▶ **If a song is too quiet**, select it, click Get Info in the File menu, and under Options boost its level using the Volume Adjustment slider. You can also do this for multiple songs at once.

▶ **If you want songs to melt into each other seamlessly**, open Preferences and, under Audio, mess around with the "Crossfade playback" settings.

▶ **iTunes can "bookmark" tracks**: remember where you'd got to so that, if you skip to another track halfway through (or switch iTunes off completely), it will return to where you left off next time you play the track in question. This is especially useful for audiobooks. To switch this feature on, select a track, choose Get Info from the File menu and check "Remember playback position" under Options.

08
Managing your music

iTunes housekeeping

A s we saw in Chapter 4 (see p.41), each song in iTunes is "tagged" with an artist name, track name and album name – information which you can either enter manually or pull off the Gracenote CD database via the Net. But, besides these three basic tagging categories, there are around twenty others, ranging from composer to sample rate – and the more info you add, the more flexibility you'll have to sort your music or create Smart Playlists. This chapter takes a brief look at tagging and managing your music – including adding cover art.

Tagging

Select a track or tracks at random and then choose Get Info from the File menu or right-click menu. In the window that will pop up, alongside the obvious bits of information, such as Artist, Title and Genre, you'll find various other fields, such as…

▶ **Equalizer,** for assigning EQ presets to specific songs (see p.122).

…and a number of boxes that really come into their own when used in conjunction with Smart Playlists (see p.73):

▶ **Comment** Use this to add whatever additional info you want about the song: the personnel playing on it, the producer, the instruments used, even lyrics if you've got the time and inclination.

▶ **Grouping** Like Comment, this is a useful wild-card category where you can create your own criteria for grouping and sorting songs. World music fans, for example, might enter a song's country of origin here; classical music fans might differentiate between century or instrument. Again, it's useful for both browsing and creating Smart Playlists.

▶ **My Rating** This is where you get to play music reviewer and enter a 0–5 star rating of each song – great if you want to create a Smart Playlist of your favourite tracks.

> ▶ TIP: You can add a rating to a track using your iPod when you are out and about. Tap the Select button twice whilst playing a song and use the scroll wheel to add a star rating. The little stars you add will find their way back into iTunes next time you sync.

▶ **BPM** Lets you specify the beats per minute of a track, which can be used to create DJ-style mixes. You could either mix tracks manually in a playlist, or sort a playlist by BPM and let iTunes do the mix with its "Crossfade" feature (see p.86). If you're into making your own music, this tag may also come in handy for picking songs of the right speed to sample.

> **TIP:** Feel free to create your own genres, rather than sticking with those in the list. If you mainly listen to jazz, say, you might want to use "bebop", "modal" and so on. Unlike when you use the Grouping field, your new genres will be easily accessible via Browse mode (see p.53).

Tagging tools

If you want to do a repetitive tagging job – move all the Grouping entries to Comment for a particular artist, say, or put the entry for Title after the entry for Artist – there's probably a script or plug-in that will automate the process. For example, try This Tag, That Tag from Doug's Apple Scripts (www.dougscripts.com).

View Options

As we've seen, one good reason for adding extra info to your tracks is to create Smart Playlists. But having extra tags also allows you extra options for viewing and sorting songs in the iTunes Song List.

By default, the Song List doesn't contain columns for most of the various information categories. But you can add and remove columns at any time using the View Options box, which can be summoned from the Edit menu or with the shortcut Apple+J (Mac) or Ctrl+J (PC). Alternatively, try Ctrl+clicking (Mac) or right-clicking (PC) the header of any of the columns in the Song List to reveal a dropdown menu of columns (as shown opposite).

Once you've checked all the columns you want to see, and unchecked those you don't, your Song List should change to reflect this. But that's not all. You can then rearrange the columns – by dragging their headers – into any order you want.

The column-header dropdown also offers the chance to "Auto Size" columns to ensure that everything in all fields is displayed. Double-clicking the division between two columns has the same result. However, this can lead to some ludicrously large columns, so it's usually better to adjust a column's width by placing your mouse pointer where two headers meet, and then dragging.

It's worth noting that these View Options are not universal, but apply only to whichever item is currently highlighted in the Source List. This is very useful, since different playlists require different fields. For a dance selection, as mentioned above, you might want to view the Beats Per Minute column, while a classical playlist would obviously need the Composer column.

Besides the track info already discussed, there are a couple of extra column options which aren't user-editable:

▶ **Play Count** The number of times a song has been played in iTunes: useful for creating Smart Playlists (such as the pre-existing iTunes "Top 25 Most Played" list).

▶ **Kind** The file format of a track (see p.111).

using iTunes & the iPod

Sorting your songs

Once you have a column in view, you can sort it by clicking its header. Click a second time and the order is reversed (with the small black triangle on the header flipping to indicate the direction of the ordering). You can jump to a particular point in the list by pressing a letter or number: if you sort by artist and press "R", say, you might jump to The Rolling Stones.

> **TIP:** The track order of a playlist is copied over to your iPod when you update. On the Pod you can't rearrange tracks, so make sure the playlists are sorted to your taste before updating.

Multiple windows

When managing and arranging your music, don't feel obliged to keep everything confined to a single iTunes panel: double-clicking a highlighted item in the Source List will open its contents in a new floating frame.

Tidying up

Every so often, check through your Library using the Browse
mode (see p.53) for artists and genres listed under two different
names – "N Cave", "Nick Cave", "Nick Cave & The Bad Seeds", for
example. Correcting these kinds of discrepancies will help to keep
your iTunes folders tidy and your Smart Playlists effective.

You can also search for duplicates in your Library – or specific
playlists – by selecting Show Duplicate Songs in the Edit menu.
Note, though, that this will only work if the artist and title info for
the two versions are identical.

Adding images

iTunes lets you add "artwork" to each track. Then, when the track
is playing or selected, it will appear in the iTunes artwork panel,
as shown below. This artwork will also appear when playing back

Clicking the fourth button below the Source List reveals/hides the artwork panel; clicking the title bar of the
panel toggles between showing artwork for the Selected Song and Now Playing song

songs on any colour-screen iPod. Most people who bother to take advantage of this feature go for the front cover of the album or single in question, which can usually be looted from the Internet. But, if you'd rather, you could choose any old picture you've found or generated. Even if you've never added any artwork, you'll probably find that you have some in your Library if you've downloaded any tracks from the iTunes Music Store (see p.143).

There are various ways to add images to a song. If you already have the image on your computer, you can drag the file directly into the artwork panel in the iTunes window, or select a track, press Apple+I (Mac) or Ctrl+I (PC), then choose Add… with the Artwork tab, and browse for the file. Alternatively, select

multiple tracks, artists or even genres, and use the same shortcut keys to open the Multiple Song Information box; then double-click the white Artwork box and locate the pic.

Mac users also have the option of dragging images straight from webpages or picture-viewing programs, and there are even iTunes plug-ins that will automatically attempt to find and download the album covers to match your songs (see p.228).

> ▶ TIP: To copy an image from a webpage, Ctrl+click (Mac) or right-click (PC) the image and select "Copy image" from the dropdown menu. Perform the same click in the iTunes Artwork window to reveal a "Paste" option.

09

Burning CDs & DVDs

creating a hard copy

As we've already seen, the playlist is the new mix tape. If you have an iPod, or your computer is hooked up to your hi-fi (see p.129), then there's little need to put your carefully compiled lists on an external medium for your own use. However, if you want to give your compilation to a friend, you'll need to burn it onto CD (or, possibly, give them the original music files; see p.158). And burning CDs and DVDs can also be a great way to back up your music. With a suitable CD or DVD drive and a copy of iTunes, none of this is very difficult.

Choices, choices

If you have a CD burner on your computer, it will usually allow you to burn two types of disc: CDR (which you can write to only once) and CDRW (which can be written to many times). You can burn to these discs in various different ways, creating:

▶ **Regular audio** CDs for playing back on standard hi-fis. These can hold around 74–80 minutes of music, depending on the disc. Use CDR, not CDRW, for burning normal music discs, as they're less likely to refuse to play back on home stereos.

▶ **MP3 CDs** can store around 10–12 hours of music, but they can only include tracks in MP3 format (see p.112) and can only be played back on computers or special MP3 CD players. Again, use CDR, not CDRW, discs.

> ▶ **TIP:** If you're using iTunes with the default settings, much of your music will be in AAC format (see p.113). If you want to burn these tracks to an MP3 CD, you'll first have to convert them to MP3. See p.119 to find out how.

▶ **Data CDs** hold music as standard computer files, so can only be read by computers and a handful of clever stereos. On the plus side, they let you store about 650–750MB of music (around 10–12 hours, depending on the sound quality) in any file format, so are useful for moving large amounts of music between computers. Both CDR and CDRW discs are good for the job.

And, if your computer has a DVD burner that's compatible with iTunes (and, in the case of Macs, a recent version of OS X), you can also create:

▶ **Data DVDs** These work just like data CDs, except that they can hold much more data (in most cases around 4.5GB) and can only be read by computers with DVD drives. Useful for backing up, these can be created on either DVDR or DVDRW discs.

To choose from these various options, open the Burning pane of the Advanced section of iTunes Preferences (see p.45). Here you can also specify a preferred burning speed: leave it set to Maximum Possible unless your machine is struggling to burn a disc successfully.

Get burning

To burn a disc in iTunes – even a data CD – you first need to arrange the relevant tracks into a playlist, as described on p.70. As you drag songs into the new list, keep an eye on the statistics at the bottom of the Song List, which will tell you the total running time and file size of the selections added so far.

Depending on the specific discs that you're going to burn, you'll need to limit yourself to around 74–80 minutes for a standard audio CD, or 650 or 700 megabytes for a data or MP3 CD. The

> **TIP:** You can also burn a CD from a Smart Playlist (see p.71). However, its contents may be different each day, so if you like the selection enough to put it on disc, burn it there and then or copy the tracks into a regular playlist to burn later.

discs or their packaging should state the capacity. If you can't resist adding more tracks than will fit on a disc, don't fret: iTunes will just burn what it can and then prompt you to insert a second disc to accommodate what's left over.

Once everything's ready, enter iTunes Preferences and, under the Burning tab (which is under Advanced), make sure you have the right kind of disc selected. If you're creating a standard audio CD, you can also choose from two extra options:

▶ **Sound Check** will alter the volume levels to equalize the loudness of the various tracks on the disc (see box opposite).

▶ **Gap Between Songs** doesn't require much explanation, though it's worth noting that these extra seconds aren't included in iTunes' estimation of the length of your playlist.

When you're ready to create your CD, select the playlist you want to burn from the Source List and then click the "Burn Disc" button in the top right corner of the iTunes window. Its little doors will rather pleasingly slide open to reveal a glowing black and yellow button and the iTunes status window will prompt you to insert a blank disc (you can insert a disc before this point, but you might find that iTunes promptly spits it out again).

You can also reach this point by selecting Burn Playlist to Disc from the File menu, or by right-clicking the playlist (Ctrl+click on a Mac) and choosing the option from the menu that pops up.

Next, iTunes checks the disc and, when it's happy asks you, via the status window, to hit the Burn Disc button once again. The

Sound Check and other options

The Sound Check function has a stab at equalizing the volume levels between tracks so that when you play back your new CD one song won't be ear-splittingly loud compared to another. This function works fine for most differences in sound level, but if you find that the songs you've combined are still irritatingly disparate on playback, try adjusting the volumes of individual tracks using the iTunes "Volume Adjustment" function (see p.127).

If that doesn't do the trick then perhaps you need to return to the source (was one song ripped from a CD and another imported from an analogue medium?) and try and figure out why a particular song has such a low noise level. Alternatively, use some audio-editing software (see p.136) to boost the volume of the quiet files.

burning process will take a few minutes, depending upon the speed of your hardware and the size of the playlist. When iTunes has finished its work it gives a little whistle, and within a few seconds your masterpiece appears in the iTunes Source List ready to be played or ejected.

> **TIP:** If you want iTunes to eject CDs automatically when they are finished, choose "Import Songs And Eject" from the "On CD Insert" menu, which lives within iTunes Preferences under Advanced/Importing. Note, though, that this also means CDs will automatically be ripped when inserted.

Burning problems

If you're having problems burning a CD or DVD using iTunes, check the following:

▶ **Is your drive supported?** Some CD and DVD drives that didn't come built in to an Apple computer are non-compatible with iTunes. But if your drive is correctly listed under Advanced/Burning in iTunes Preferences, it should theoretically be fine.

▶ **Are the songs you are trying to burn protected?** Songs purchased from the iTunes Music Store are only burnable a certain number of times – perhaps the tracks you are trying to burn have already exceeded their burn privileges. If this is the case, find the CD that already features the songs (assuming you didn't post it to some distant relative) and re-import the tracks in an unprotected format.

▶ **Are you burning the right type of files?** If burning an MP3 CD, you can only include songs in the MP3 format. Turning on the Kind column in the Song List lets you see which tracks are in which format. Also see the Tip Box on p.96.

▶ **Have the songs in your playlist been authorized?** If songs purchased from the iTunes Music Store have not been authorized to play on your computer, CD burning will not work. Double-click the songs in the Song List and enter the ID and password for the account with which the songs were purchased. You may additionally need to deauthorize another computer if you have exceeded the maximum number of computers authorized to play the tracks (see p.148).

▶ **Does your computer go to sleep while you burn?** To stop this from happening in OS X, open System Preferences and within the Energy Saver pane increase the time before your computer sleeps. On a PC this is done in the Control Panel under Power Management.

▶ **Are you trying to play the wrong type of CD?** If you have successfully created a CD but it won't work on one or more hi-fis, double-check that you are burning a regular audio CD (see p.96) onto a CDR disc (not CDRW). Still, even if you did everything right, some CD players (especially older ones) will refuse all computer-generated CDs.

Making covers

Half the joy of assembling a compilation has always been the painstaking process of making the cover. Doing this on a computer may not have the same romance about it, but at least you don't have to manually write out all the artist and track names – and with a half-decent printer you can create some pretty professional-looking results.

With iTunes

To create a cover using the iTunes built-in tools, select the playlist that you've just burned – or choose a genre, artist or album in Browse mode – and select Print from the File menu. Alternatively, hit the keyboard shortcut Apple+P (Mac) or Ctrl+P (PC). A box will pop up offering you various options for printing the details of the playlist's contents as either a regular document or an insert for a CD jewel case – each with a number of options relating to the layout of track names and any available artwork. If and when you are happy with how the cover or sheet looks (you can get a

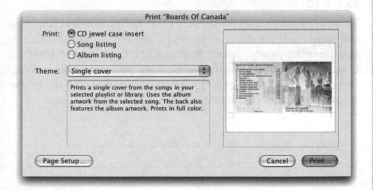

101

full-sized view by clicking Print and then Preview), choose Page Setup to assign printer-specific options and then hit Print.

Other programs

This is all very handy, but rather artistically limiting. Another option is to export your playlist's track names as a text document, and then paste them into another program that will allow you more creativity over the cover. To do this, select a playlist and then choose Export Playlist... from the File and right-click menus. A box appears where you can choose to save the file as a text document or an XML document.

> **TIP:** Whatever software you intend to use to make your covers – be it Microsoft Word or something more graphically serious, such as Adobe Creative Suite – you should be able to find various CD templates ready to download and fill in online. Searching Google for "CD", "templates" and the name of your program should lead you to them.

Extra tools

There are a number of third-party tools and scripts that can help you create CD covers. For example, the free iTunes Publisher (available from www.trancesoftware.com) lets you export playlists in various formats, including tabbed text, Winamp and HTML. Or try the "Playlist to papercdcase.com" script from Doug's Apple Scripts For iTunes (www.dougscripts.com).

10
Sharing
music
a little give and take

I n the world of digitized music, the term "sharing" is slightly ambiguous. It can refer to uncontentious software features such as the "sharing" functions of iTunes, which allow you to listen to music stored on other computers on your home or office network. It can also refer to highly controversial practices, such as exchanging vast swathes of music with friends – the kind of thing that prompts the music industry to claim that there's no distinction between sharing copyrighted music and stealing it. This chapter looks at both these areas; for information about Internet-based peer-2-peer file sharing, see p.157.

iTunes sharing over a network

A network is two or more computers connected together, either with cables or a wireless technology such as Wi-Fi (AirPort in Mac-speak). If you have more than one computer in the house, networking them together allows you to share files, printers and an Internet connection. If each computer is equipped with iTunes, a network also lets you "stream" music from one to another, with each computer having access to the music stored on the others – even between Macs and PCs. These days, setting up a home network can take seconds rather than days; for more info, see *The Rough Guide to the Internet*, *The Rough Guide to PCs & Windows* and *The Rough Guide to Macs & OS X*.

> **TIP:** Sharing music over a network with iTunes has certain limitations: you can't copy or burn music from other computers, nor add it to your iPod. And the computers have to be switched on to be accessible. If you'd rather permanently copy music files from machine to machine, see p.106.

Start sharing

First of all you'll need to set the sharing options for each computer on the network. Open iTunes Preferences (see p.45) and, under the Sharing tab, you'll see two main checkboxes: "Look for shared music" (which instructs iTunes to find shared music on other com-

puters on the network) and "Share my music" (which breaks down further into sharing your entire Library or just selected specified playlists). As for the "Shared name" box, whatever you enter here will pop up in the Source List of other users on the network.

Next, decide if you want to set a password for others accessing your songs: this option is not compulsory, but it could be useful if, say, you're embarrassed about your easy listening playlist. When you are done, click OK and start sharing.

> TIP: Songs purchased from the iTunes Music Store can only be shared on up to five authorized machines due to DRM restrictions (see p.148).

Listening to shared music

Once you've set up two computers to share, their icons should appear in each other's Source List. Click the icon, entering the sharer's password if required, and you can browse these selections either directly from the Song List or by clicking the small triangle to the left of the shared music icon to reveal any playlists on the shared computer. Double-click a song and then sit back and listen as the streaming starts.

> **TIP:** To check whether the songs you are browsing are your own or shared, use the Kind column of the Song List (see p.91). Shared files will appear with the word "remote" in brackets after the format type.

Disconnecting

When you've finished with someone else's Library you "eject" it in the same way that you do a CD or your iPod: either hit the icon to the right of the shared music icon in the Source List, or hit the eject button in the bottom right of the iTunes window.

Copying music from computer-to-computer

The other way to share your music is to literally move the relevant files from your iPod or computer to someone else's computer. It probably goes without saying that ripping a massive library of tracks from copyrighted CDs and then donating it to all your friends is against the law. But there are legitimate reasons for this kind of copying: you might have two computers in the same house, say, or be upgrading to a new machine. You might also be copying music you've downloaded from the iTunes Music Store, in which case you're allowed to authorize a certain number of other computers to play each track.

As described on p.222, there is software available – not supported by Apple – that will allow you to pull music directly from your iPod onto any computer running iTunes. However, it's far easier and more reliable to copy the files from computer to computer.

First of all, you need to locate the music you want to copy, selecting either your whole iTunes folder (see p.51), certain artist folders within it, or individual tracks or albums within those.

Next, you need to move those folders or files to an empty folder (not directly to the iTunes folder) on the other computer. This can be done in various ways…

▶ **Over a network** If the computers in question are already on the same network, you can enable file sharing and simply copy the artist folders you want directly from one machine to another. File sharing may already be on: if not, on a Mac, open System Preferences and look under Sharing; on a PC, right-click the iTunes folder and select Sharing and Security. For more details, search Windows or Mac OS X Help.

▶ **Via an iPod or external hard drive** If you have an external hard drive (see p.232) you can back up your iTunes Music folder to it and then copy the files across to the other computer. If you don't have an external drive but you do have an iPod, you could enable the iPod as a hard disk (see p.167) and use it to copy across the files.

> TIP: Copying files over a network and via a CD/DVD should work fine between a PC and a Mac. However, if using a hard drive or iPod, a PC won't be able to read the drive or Pod if it was formatted on a Mac (see p.172).

▶ **On a CD or DVD** As explained in the previous chapter, when you burn a "data CD" (as opposed to a regular audio CD), you can fit around ten hours of music on it. A DVD can hold more like sixty hours.

Importing the files

Once you have the files on the target computer, you'll need to import them into iTunes in the usual way. See p.52.

Serious about sound

11
Music file formats
balancing sound quality and disk space

As we've already seen, importing from CD is a cinch. However, if you care about the sound quality or transferability of your music archive, you'll want to investigate the various import options. These allow you to weigh up the size of the imported music files against the fidelity of the sound and the degree to which they'll be compatible with software and hardware other than iTunes and the iPod. This chapter focuses on importing from CD, but the advice applies equally to files you've downloaded or created yourself.

serious about sound

Importing options

To access the iTunes Importing options, open iTunes Preferences (see p.45), click the Advanced button and choose the Importing tab. The two most important options are those in the drop-downs. They allow you to choose which file format/ compression type to use, and the bitrate. If you're not sure what a file format or bitrate is, read on.

> TIP: One minor problem with bigger, higher-quality music files is that, when played on an iPod, they use slightly more battery power each second when played.

Which format?

iTunes currently offers five file-format import options: AAC, MP3, AIFF, Apple Lossless and WAV. If any of these don't appear in your list of options, you're probably running an old version of iTunes. Download and install the latest version (see p.40).

The box opposite explains the pros, cons and uses of each format. But, in brief, AAC is best for day-to-day iPod and computer use; MP3 is slightly worse at the same bitrate, but can be played on any digital music player or computer (and burned onto MP3

MP3, AAC and other import options

MP3 [Moving Pictures Experts Group-1/2 Audio Layer 3]
MP3 is the most common format for storing music on computer and digital music players – by quite a long way. That gives it one great advantage: if you import your music as MP3s, you can be safe in the knowledge that it will be transferable to any other player or software that you might use in the future, or which friends and family may already own. However, it no longer provides the best sound-quality/disk-space balance.
File name ends: .mp3
Use it for: importing music you want to be able to share with non-iPod people and players, and for burning CDs to play on special MP3 CD players.

AAC [Advanced Audio Coding]
This is a relatively new encoding format, which is being pushed by Apple for two reasons. First, according to the general consensus, AAC sounds noticeably better than MP3 when recorded at the same bitrate. Second, AAC allows Apple to embed their own DRM technology (see p.145) into files downloaded from the iTunes Music Store, to stop people freely distributing the files (MP3 DRM is a very recent phenomenon).
File name ends: .m4a (standard), **.m4p** (when DRM is included)
Use it for: importing music you don't expect to share with non-iPod people and players.

Apple Lossless Encoder
A recent Apple innovation, this format offers full CD quality, but only consumes around half the disk space – expect to fit between three and five albums per gigabyte. Currently the format only works on iTunes and iPods.
File name ends: .ale
Use it for: importing music at the highest quality for computer or iPod use. Note, though, that it won't work with an iPod shuffle.

AIFF [Advanced Interchange File Format], **WAV** [Wave]
These uncompressed formats offer the same quality as the newer Apple Lossless Encoder but they take up twice as much disk space (and won't play back on an iPod shuffle). In their favour, they can be played on nearly any computer software and also imported into audio-editing programs. Also, you might find that CDs import slightly more quickly than with Apple Lossless.
File name ends: .aiff, .wav
Use it for: importing music for burning onto CD and then deleting, or for editing with audio software, but not for general iTunes or Pod playback.

CDs); Apple Lossless is for fidelity fanatics; and AIFF and WAV are only really for importing tracks with the aim of burning CDs.

Note that all file formats can be burned to audio CDs and played back in normal hi-fis – it's only when sharing actual music files with non-iTunes or non-iPod equipment that compatibility becomes an issue.

> TIP: It's fine to mix different file formats and bitrates in your Library. Indeed, this is a sensible plan as some kinds of music will receive little benefit from high-bitrate encoding. Very sludgy, stoner-type rock, for example, may not require the same fidelity as a carefully regulated Fazioli grand piano.

Which bitrate?

As already explained (see p.21), the bitrate is the amount of data that each second of sound is reduced to. The higher the bitrate, the higher the sound quality, but also the more disk space the track takes up. The relationship between file size and bitrate is basically proportional, but the same isn't true of sound quality, so a 128 Kbps track takes half as much space as the same track recorded at 256 Kbps, but the sound will be only very marginally different. Still, marginal differences are what being a hi-fi obsessive is all about.

The default import setting in recent versions of iTunes, listed as "high quality", is AAC at 128 Kbps. Most people will be perfectly satisfied with this combination (which is usually said to be roughly equivalent to MP3 at 160 Kbps), but if you're into your sound in a serious way it may not be quite good enough. Particularly if you listen to high-fidelity recordings of acoustic instruments, such as well-recorded classical music, and if you connect your iPod or computer to a decent home stereo (see p.129), you may find AAC 128 Kbps leads to a distinct lack of presence and brightness in your favourite recordings. If so, either opt for the Apple Lossless Encoder (see p.113) or stick with AAC and up the bitrate. The best thing to do is to run a comparative experiment with a suitably well-recorded track (see box below).

Running a soundcheck

The only reliable way to determine the right sound quality for your own ear, headphones and hi-fi is to do a comparative experiment. Launch iTunes and insert a CD you consider to be as detailed and clear in its recording quality as anything in your collection. Pick one track that sounds particularly hi-fi and uncheck the rest of the tracks. Name it "Soundcheck ALE" in the Song List, since you will be importing this at CD quality using Apple Lossless format. Open iTunes Preferences and select the Apple Lossless option within Advanced/Importing. Import the track.

Next, return to the CD in the Source List, rename the track "Soundcheck 128 AAC", select the AAC 128 Kbps option from Preferences, and import the track again. Do this again at various other AAC and/or MP3 bitrates – say 160, 224 and 320 Kbps – each time renaming the track so it's easy to locate.

Once you're done, plug in your iPod, transfer the tracks across, and then do some comparative listening either on headphones or, ideally, connected through a decent home stereo and speaker system (see p.129). Then you can make an informed decision about which format is right for you.

115

serious about sound

Tweaking the settings

When setting the bitrate, the "Custom" option reveals a panel full of techie settings relating to frequencies and the like. You can safely ignore most of these, though it's worth knowing about one or two, as they may help you to strike a better balance between file size and sound quality.

Channels

With mono encoding there is only one "channel" of music within the file, which, when played, is duplicated to both your left and right earphones or speakers. Stereo encoding produces a two-channel file, which gives you a distinct sound in both left and right speakers and creates file sizes double those of mono. The Joint Stereo option reduces the file size of normal stereo slightly by combining parts of the two channels where possible. Podcasts

LAME MP3 encoding

Just as there's more than one way to skin a cat, there's also more than one way to encode an MP3 file. The encoder built into iTunes does a decent-enough job, but there are alternatives out there that arguably do it better. Indeed, there's a near-consensus among people who are interested in such

```
000            iTunes-LAME
--alt-preset standard        ▼ ✓  [📲]
           Encoding Options      Import
        Importing: "Colours 2"        ⊗
        Time Remaining: 0:50 (4.8x)
        ▬▬▬▬▬▬▬▬▬▬▬▬▬▬
              Track 1 of 4
                   [?]  [Prefs]  [About]
```

things that the best MP3 encoder for files with a bitrate of 128 Kbps or higher is an open-source (non-copyrighted) one known as LAME. (Its somewhat self-deprecating name stands, bizarrely enough, for "LAME Ain't an MP3 Encoder".)

Mac users who fancy getting the audiophile benefits of LAME can grab the easy-to-use **iTunes-LAME** script (www.blacktree.com/apps/iTunes-LAME), which adds LAME encoding to iTunes via the Scripts menu. Once installed, you can use LAME when importing tracks from a CD, and also when converting songs into MP3 from other formats. If you have a PC, you'll find various free programs featuring LAME encoding at lame.sourceforge.net/links.html, though at the time of writing none of them integrate quite so neatly with iTunes.

(see p.163) are often encoded in either mono or joint stereo to keep their file size down.

Variable Bit Rate Encoding

When switched on, VBR varies the bitrate in real time, according to the complexity of the sound. With some music, this can save quite a lot of disk space.

Smart Encoding Adjustments

If you select Smart Encoding Adjustments, then iTunes will automatically select what it thinks are the most appropriate settings for any options that you've left set to Auto.

Filter Frequencies Below 10Hz

Frequencies below 10Hz are inaudible to humans, so removing them should reduce the size of your files without affecting the sound. But try a test file before making this your default setting, as some audiophiles have commented that removing these frequencies can result in an unbalanced sound and even the appearance of a tinnitus-like ringing in the recording.

WMA, Audible & Ogg Vorbis

Beside those formats listed on p.113, there are various others that you may come across – some of which iTunes and the iPod can handle and some of which they can't. Two of the most common are:

▶ **Windows Media** (.wma) If these have embedded DRM protection, iTunes won't touch them – unless you burn an audio CD of the tracks and re-rip it in another format. If, however, they're not DRM-protected, iTunes will simply create an AAC copy of them in your Library.

▶ **Audible** (.aa) This is a special format designed to sound good for spoken word – audio books, for example – at extremely low bitrates, but it isn't used for music. It's fully compatible with iTunes and iPods. For more, see p.200.

Terms like MP3 are so ubiquitous that it's easy to assume they're common property, but in fact nearly all such technologies are the intellectual assets of companies, which charge other companies (such as software manufacturers) to use them. Somewhere along the line, consumers foot the bill and profits may come before other considerations.

Increasingly, however, where there's a commercial piece of software there's also a free alternative produced by the open-source programming community (best known for the Linux operating system). And, true to form, the open-source crew have developed their own "patent-and-royalty-free" format:

▶ **Ogg Vorbis** (.ogg) is often claimed to sound better than any other format (visit www.vorbis.com if you "dare to compare"). At the time of writing, Apple hasn't included Ogg Vorbis support into iPod. If you'd like to see them do so, drop Apple a line and let them know. In the meantime, it is possible to get Ogg Vorbis files to work within iTunes using the QuickTime Component available from www.xiph.org/quicktime.

Converting one format to another

iTunes allows you to change tracks easily from one format to another. This can sometimes be very useful: if you have any bulky WAV or AIFF files sitting around in your Library, for example, you can massively reduce the disk space they take up by converting them to Apple Lossless, AAC or MP3 format. And the resulting file will be as good as if you'd ripped it straight from CD.

Be warned, however, that re-encoding files that are already in MP3, AAC or some other compressed format is in general a bad idea. Each file format works by removing different things from the sound file, so even if MP3 and AAC both sound great, a track that has undergone both compressions may sound noticeably worse.

You may sometimes think this is a price worth paying: if you have an archive of high-bitrate MP3s, for example, and you want to save disk space by reducing them to lower-bitrate AACs; or if you have a high-bitrate spoken-word recording that you're happy to reduce in quality. But before deleting the original versions be sure to carefully compare the sound through some decent head-phones or a hi-fi and see if you're satisfied with the results.

To convert a track, first specify your desired format and bitrate under Importing options (within iTunes Preferences, under Advanced). Then select the file or files in question and

> ▶ TIP: If you're a hi-fi buff with plenty of computer disk space, consider importing your CDs using Apple Lossless for use through your stereo (see p.129) but creating an AAC copy of each for use on your iPod, where disk space is more limited. After you've created the copies, simply create a Smart Playlist (see p.71) that finds all MP3 and AAC files, and set your Pod to automatically update that playlist only (see p.57).

serious about sound

choose Convert selection to… from the Advanced or right-click menus. Then, if you're sure, delete the original (see p.55).

If iTunes won't let you convert a file, it may have embedded DRM protection (see p.16). You may be able to get around this by putting the file on a standard audio CD (see p.96) and then re-ripping it in a different format. However, this may break the terms of your user licence, depending on where you got the track. The same is true of the various converting programs that you can easily find online.

For more info, see: www.mp3-converter.com

> **TIP:** If you download and install an iTunes update, your import file format may default to Apple's AAC; if you prefer to import with a different format, change it back within Preferences under Importing.

12

Tweaking the sound

EQ and beyond

As we've seen, one way to enhance the sound on your computer and iPod is to be discerning with your importing preferences (see p.112). Another option is to improve your speakers, either by investing in better earphones for your Pod (see p.216) or by hooking up to a decent hi-fi (see p.129). But aside from all this, you can also tweak the sound using various iTunes tools, including a pretty comprehensive graphic equalizer. You can either apply EQ as you listen or assign customized presets to specific tracks, which are then transported to your iPod when you next plug it in.

serious about sound

Equalizing

The iTunes Equalizer allows you to adjust a range of frequency bands (see box opposite) for the music coming out of your computer. To open Equalizer, hit its stripy button in the lower right corner of the iTunes pane.

First make sure the Equalizer is active by checking the box in the top left of the pane. Note, though, that this window doesn't need to be open for the settings to be having an effect – you can tell whether the Equalizer is currently active by seeing whether its button in the main iTunes window is glowing blue.

> TIP: On a Mac, you can also open Equalizer from the iTunes Window menu or by using the keyboard shortcut Apple+2.

A Rough Guide to EQ

All music, all sound in fact, is made up of vibrations at various different frequencies, which are expressed in hertz – cycles per second. Deep bass sounds are produced at low frequencies (as little as 32 hertz), while very high-pitched sounds come from much higher frequencies (perhaps 16 kilohertz, which means 16,000 cycles per second). All other audible sound lies somewhere in between.

Music, especially when produced by acoustic instruments, consists of an astonishingly complex and dynamic combination of different frequencies. And to get the optimum sound, you need to tweak the relative volume of the different frequencies according to your taste, your speakers, the recording quality and even the shape of the room you're in.

Most stereos offer the option to boost or suppress the loudness of high and low frequencies under the broad titles of "treble" and "bass". However, given that a range of frequencies could be divided into an infinite number of "bands", each of which could then be individually tweaked, there is scope for far more precision. In the world of hi-fi hardware, this precision is supplied by graphic equalizers, which offer a panel of sliders for adjusting the volume of various different frequency bands – changing the "EQ" of the overall sound. As explained overleaf, iTunes offers something very similar, but more flexible.

Presets

From the dropdown menu you can choose between a number of preset frequency settings, designed to suit different types of music: the "Dance" preset, for example, has a heavier bass setting, while the "Spoken Word" setting features stronger mid-range frequencies, just like the human voice. Play some music that you are familiar with and try a few of the presets, even ones that don't sound at all suitable from their name. Take a look at the different shapes that the Equalizer's sliders make on-screen and get a feel for what is happening to the music. Toggle the tick-box in the Equalizer panel "on" and "off" to compare your new settings to the unequalized version of the song.

serious about sound

Make your own presets

At any time you can drag the sliders up and down yourself to try and get a sound perfectly matched to the music you're listening to (as you do so, the Preset dropdown will display Manual). If you create an EQ that you like, you can save it by selecting "Make Preset…" from the dropdown and choosing a name.

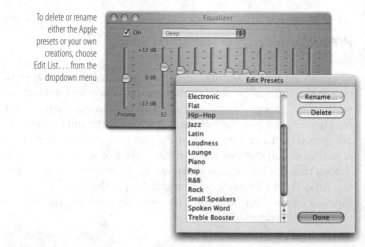

Once you've made a preset, you can recall its particular combination of levels by clicking its entry in the dropdown menu. Or you can edit or rename the presets, as shown below.

To delete or rename either the Apple presets or your own creations, choose Edit List… from the dropdown menu

Make Preset

New Preset Name:
My new EQ

Cancel   OK

Edit Presets

Electronic
Flat
Hip-Hop
Jazz
Latin
Loudness
Lounge
Piano
Pop
R&B
Rock
Small Speakers
Spoken Word
Treble Booster

Rename…
Delete

Done

> **TIP:** When constructing your own EQ presets, start with
> the "Flat" preset and build on that: you'll get a much
> better feel for the effect each of your additional drags is
> having on the original sound.

EQing songs

So far we've looked at using the Equalizer as a real-time tool,
simply changing the settings and presets as you listen. But iTunes
can do more than that: using the song information panels, the
program allows you to associate preset EQs with individual songs
so that both iTunes and your iPod know exactly how you want to
hear them.

First, in the Song List select the song, or songs, you want to add
an EQ preset to and then choose "Get Info" from the File menu.
Now simply choose the preset you want to use from the Equalizer
Preset dropdown menu
(found under Options
when you are dealing
with a single song).

serious about sound

> TIP: If boosting individual frequency bands with
> the Equalizer causes the sound to distort, lower the
> Preamp setting to between −6db and −12db, and then
> compensate by increasing your computer's master volume level.

And on to the Pod...

All your Equalizer presets and individual song associations are
carried over to the iPod when you update, though you can manually select the preset you want to use from the EQ menu within
the iPod's main Settings menu. This is also the place to go to toggle the iPod's Sound Check function "on" and "off". However, the
single best way to improve the sound that comes out of your iPod
is to buy a good pair of sound-isolating headphones (see p.216).

Other sound settings

Other than EQs, iTunes offers a couple of other sound-tweaking
settings within the Playback pane of iTunes Preferences...

Sound Enhancer

In theory, when you set
the Sound Enhancer to
high you should notice
a general improvement
of the "presence" in the
music you play. It's tricky
to quantify, but the sound
should be brighter and the
stereo separation really
vivid. You may not like the

effect – or not be able to tell the difference – but it's certainly worth experimenting with, so check the box, slide the slider and see what you think.

Sound Enhancer is usually most beneficial for compressed audio formats like MP3 and AAC, but you may also notice a difference with CD playback. The only real downside is that it can keep your computer's processor pretty busy, which could result in glitches and skips if you don't have a fast machine.

Sound Check

When Sound Check is on, iTunes attempts to play back songs at approximately the same volume level, so you shouldn't have to keep turning the sound up and down as you jump around your collection. As more songs are added to your Library, iTunes recalculates its setting and stores the information in its database. It's not perfect, and you may still notice discrepancies in loudness between different songs, expecially where songs have been imported from a non-CD source. If particular tracks are still too quiet or loud, use the Volume Adjustment (see box) setting to bring them into line.

Volume Adjustment

To boost or lower the volume of a particular track, select it – or them – in the Song List and choose Get Info from the FIle menu. In the box that pops up, under Options, use the Volume Adjustment slider to alter the volume of that specific song. iTunes remembers the new setting and will use it whenever the song is played. You can do this for multiple tracks – or even whole genres, artists or albums in Browse mode (see p.53).

Third-party plug-ins

The iTunes sound features are pretty good, but if you want even more you'll find plenty of free or inexpensive programs on the Net. Among the best is Volume Logic. Available for both Mac and PC, this little application presents level meters, a plethora of "sound checking" and EQing functions, and a handsome little panel that integrates with iTunes very snugly.

Volume Logic www.octiv.com

13

Hooking up to hi-fis

playing through ...
recording from

The iPod does an excellent job of putting your music collection in your pocket. But when you want to listen at home, a pair of earphones is not ideal. Neither, for that matter, are tinny little computer speakers. There are various special iPod-speaker options (see pp.213–215), though the ideal solution is to hook up your iPod, your computer, or both, to a decent hi-fi – something that can be done in a number of ways. Besides the obvious advantages in sound quality, marrying your computer and hi-fi also allows you to get music from vinyl, cassette and radio into your iTunes Library and onto your Pod.

serious about sound

Playing through a hi-fi

To get the sound from your Pod or computer into your hi-fi, the latter should ideally have an available line-in channel – look on the back for an unused pair of red and white RCA sockets. They may be labelled "Aux" or "Line-in", though any input other than Phono (which will have a built-in preamp) should be fine.

If your hi-fi doesn't have a line-in, but it does have a radio, you could consider an FM transmitter (see p.134). If it does have a line-in, you have a number of options…

Connecting with cables

Computer to hi-fi

Nearly all computers have line-out and/or headphone capabilities – usually in the form of a single 3.5mm "minijack" socket. So if your computer and stereo share a desk or are only a few feet apart, you can easily pick up an RCA-to-minijack cable (pictured) and run it straight from the computer to the hi-fi's line-in. (Some computers have RCA line-outs as well as a minijack, in which case you can use a standard RCA-to-RCA cable.)

When buying a cable, check all the plugs are "male" not "female" (they probably will be) and, if you can, spend a little extra to get gold-plated jacks – they deliver a far cleaner sound.

If your computer and hi-fi are further apart or in different rooms, you could buy a long cable and get the drill out, but you might prefer to investigate AirPort Express (see p.132).

> TIP: If no signal seems to be getting to your stereo from iTunes, make sure that your volume is turned up both in the program and on your system's master volume.

iPod to hi-fi

One problem with running your computer through your hi-fi is that you need to have your computer on to hear anything, which can be a pain if your machine takes ages to boot up or has a noisy cooling fan. You might find it more convenient to attach your iPod instead. A Pod doesn't give you quite the ease of use and flexibility of iTunes, but it's small, silent and doesn't require you to run a cable across your room.

Simply run an RCA-to-minijack cable between your hi-fi's line-in and your Pod's headphone socket or, much better, the "Line Out" on the back of the Dock, as pictured here. The Dock solution can be made all the more convenient when combined with a wireless remote control (see p.218).

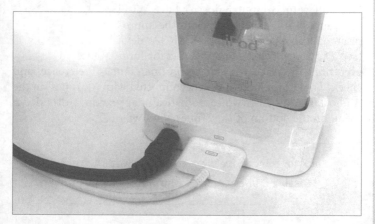

Connecting wirelessly

AirTunes

If your hi-fi has a line-in socket, but you don't want to be limited by cables – perhaps you have a laptop or your computer is in a different room from your stereo – investigate Apple's AirPort Express wireless base station (pictured), with its so-called AirTunes feature.

Attach one of these to a power point near to your hi-fi and connect it to the stereo with a standard RCA-to-minijack cable. Then, any computer with Wi-Fi capability – known as AirPort on a Mac – can beam music straight from iTunes to the hi-fi, even from the other side of the house. If your computer doesn't have Wi-Fi you can add it inexpensively with the appropriate internal, external or PCMCIA device (see *The Rough Guide to the Internet* for more). Once everything's in place, you can simply open iTunes Preferences and check "Look for remote speakers connected with AirTunes" in the Audio tab. Your hi-fi will automatically appear in a dropdown menu on the bottom of the iTunes window.

☑ **Look for remote speakers connected with AirTunes**
☐ **Disable iTunes volume control for remote speakers**

Other wireless music receivers

The kind of Wi-Fi streaming technology described opposite is not exclusive to AirTunes. There are many other devices that do a similar job, integrate with iTunes and boast additional features, such as a display, Ethernet ports, Internet radio streaming and remote controls. Once again, however, songs purchased from the iTunes Music Store won't work with non-Apple equipment unless you go to the hassle of burning and re-ripping them (see p.156).

▶ **Squeezebox** www.slimdevices.com (pictured)
▶ **SoundBridge** www.rokulabs.com
▶ **HomePod** www.macsense.com

AirPort Express can also beam an Internet connection around your house, and allow you to connect to printers wirelessly (for more information, see: www.apple.com/airportexpress) and with a third-party application such as Airfoil you can also use your AirPort Express to stream audio from other applications as well as iTunes – whether it be a web browser, another media player, or one of the audio editors we describe on p.136.

▶ **Airfoil** www.rogueamoeba.com/airfoil $25 (Mac & PC)

> ▶ TIP: For a really minimal wireless music system, unencumbered by such old-fashion equipment as a hi-fi, combine an AirPort Express with a pair of powered speakers (see p.215).

serious about sound

FM transmitters

An FM transmitter plugs into the headphone socket on your iPod (many will also plug into a computer) and beams the sound around the room as an FM radio signal. Then your stereo can tune in just as it would any other radio station. Though you won't get CD fidelity and your stereo or iPod will need to be relatively close to your radio, this is a very convenient solution, allowing you to walk around the house zapping music from your Pod to any nearby radio. It's also the only easy way to connect to a hi-fi that lacks a line-in socket. For recommended models, see p.206.

TIP: As well as connecting to your home hi-fi, it's possible to connect to the one in your car. For more on this, see p.206 and p.211.

Bluetooth transmitters

Connect a Bluetooth transmitter to your iPod and a matching receiver to your stereo's spare RCA inputs, and you can beam music across the room. The sound quality is much higher with Bluetooth than with FM radio, but then so is the price tag.

The most popular model at the time of writing is the Griffin BlueTrip (see www.griffintechnology.com/products/bluetrip).

Recording music from a hi-fi

Other than playing music through a home stereo speaker system, the other reason you might want to connect your computer to a hi-fi is to "rip" analogue sound sources – vinyl, cassettes, even a radio programme – into a digital file format. You can't record directly into the iPod this way, but anything you record onto your computer can then be transferred onto your Pod.

Audio interfaces

Though most computers do feature line-in sockets, some – such as Apple's iBook – don't. But there are loads of pieces of USB hardware on the market that will provide you with a basic line-in and mic-in socket (such as Griffin's iMic, pictured) or, if your budget allows, a more professional selection of studio-quality ports and sockets.

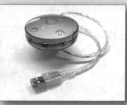

iMic www.griffintechnology.com/products/imic

For insight, advice and details and reviews of other possibilities, try:

PC Music Guru (PCs and Macs) www.pcmusic.com
SilentWay.com (Macs) www.silentway.com/tips

Getting analogue sound into your iTunes Library is more time-consuming than ripping from CD – and more difficult to get right in terms of sound quality. You will have to set the levels right, record the album or track in "real time" into some audio recording software (see p.136), and then mess around with filters and effects to clean up the sound. So if you can find a CD reissue or a MP3 version of the track online, that's probably the best option. But for those tracks that can't easily be found in digital format, here's what to do…

Stage 1: Hooking up

First of all, you'll need to make the right connection. With any luck, your computer will have a line-in or mic port, probably in the form of a minijack socket (if it doesn't you can add one with the right USB device; see box above). On the hi-fi, a headphone socket will suffice, but you'll get a much better "level" from a dedicated line-out – check on the back of the system for a pair of

RCA sockets labelled "Line Out", "Tape Out" or something similar. That way, also, you'll only need a standard RCA-to-minijack cable – which you might even already have.

> TIP: You're not limited to household hi-fis. With the right cable you can record from any device with a headphone jack – including Walkmans, MiniDisc players and portable radios.

Stage 2: Check you have enough disk space

During the actual recording process, you'll need plenty of hard-drive space: as much as a gigabyte for an album, or 15MB per minute. (Once you've finished recording, you can convert the music that you've imported into a space-efficient format such as MP3 or AAC, and delete the giant original.)

Stage 3: Choose some software

Recording from analogue sources requires an audio recording application. You may already have something suitable on your computer, but there are scores of excellent programs available to download off the Net. Here are a few recommendations:

▶ **Audacity (Mac & PC)** audacity.sourceforge.net
With Audacity you can record and edit WAV, AIFF, Ogg Vorbis and MP3 files, and more. As well as built-in effects it features an unlimited undo function – very useful. Best of all, it's free.

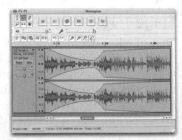

▶ **Garageband (Mac)** www.apple.com/iLife
Part of Apple's iLife multimedia suite (roughly $80/£50, or
bundled free with new Macs), Garageband is an easy-to-use
multitrack recording studio well suited to ripping tracks from
analogue sources. Though it lacks a wealth of filters, its intuitive
layout makes it an attractive option.

▶ **AudioGrabber (PC)** www.audiograbber.com
This excellent freeware features normalizing (see p.139) and
sound-enhancing tools. Supports Ogg Vorbis among others.

▶ **Auqio Sound Studio (PC)** www.auqio.com
Though it costs around $100/£60, this program offers a plethora
of recording and editing tools.

▶ **CD Spin Doctor (Mac)** www.roxio.com/toast
Part of Roxio's CD-burning package Toast (roughly $80/£50),
Spin Doctor allows you to record audio, clean and enhance
sound quality, and create MP3 files ready to slip into iTunes.

serious about sound

For many more audio software options, including freebies, point your Web browser at:

AudioMelody www.audiomelody.com
Shareware Music Machine www.hitsquad.com/smm
Tucows www.tucows.com

> ▶ TIP: Audio-editing software isn't just for recording. It can also come in useful for trimming, cutting up, editing or combining tracks in your iTunes Library.

Stage 4: Recording…

Connect your computer and hi-fi as described above, and switch your hi-fi's amplifier to "Phono", "Tape" or whichever channel you're recording from. Launch your audio recorder and open a new file. The details from here on in vary according to which program you're running and the analogue source you are recording from, but roughly speaking the procedure is the same.

You'll be asked to specify a few parameters for the new recording. The defaults (usually 44.1kHz, 16-bit stereo) should be fine. Play the loudest section of the record to get an idea of the maximum level. A visual meter should display the sound coming in – you want as much level as possible *without* hitting the red.

If you seem to be getting little or no level, make sure your line-in is specified as your recording channel and the input volume is up: on a Mac, look under Sound in System Preferences; on a PC, check the line-in in Sound and Multimedia in the Control Panel, and the level by opening Volume Controls (Start Menu/Programs/Accessories/Entertainment), clicking Properties in the Options menu, selecting Recording and pressing OK.

When you're ready, press "Record" and start your vinyl, cassette or whatever, playing. When the song or album is finished, press

"Stop". A graphic wave form will appear on the screen. Use the "cut" tool to tidy up any extraneous noise or blank space from the beginning and end of the file; fade in and out to hide the "cuts".

> **TIP:** If you're recording from vinyl, make sure the turntable is connected to a stereo amplifier through either a dedicated "phono" port or a separate preamplifier. This is important as vinyl is often cut with bass and treble frequencies reversed to decrease the need for an overly wide or deep groove. Preamplifiers and phono ports correct this inverted equalization, boost the levels, and generally stop the signal sounding tinny.

Stage 5: Tidying up the sound

It won't always be necessary, but it's often a good idea – especially if you're recording from vinyl – to try and clean up the sound a bit. Your audio editor may offer hiss, pop and crackle filters, or for serious projects you could try a dedicated noise reduction program, such as SoundSoap (www.bias-inc.com). However, don't go clean-up mad and don't overwrite your original file until you get just the right sound: removing hiss and crackle is good, but if you end up with a recording that lacks the warmth or presence of the shellac version, you'll be disappointed.

If there's a "normalize" function you could also use this to maximize the level without distorting it. This will ensure that, if you rip a number of tracks, they will all end up at the same volume level.

Stage 6: Convert the file

When you are happy with what you've got, save the file in WAV or AIFF format, and perhaps back it up to CD. Then import the

serious about sound

file into iTunes (choose Import... from the File menu), convert it to a compressed format of your choice (see p.113) and delete the bulky original from both your iTunes folder (see p.55) and its original location.

Your masterful remaster is now ready to be played back on iTunes or uploaded to your Pod.

Read on

The finer details of recording and editing audio can take a lifetime to master. If you want good results, or you get stuck, do some reading online, starting with:

OSXAudio www.osxaudio.com
PC Music Guru www.pc-music.com

 TIP: If you have money to spare, an easier way to get your vinyl into iTunes is to invest in a USB turntable, such as the ION USB.

Music
online

14

iTunes Music Store

the Apple option

A s the following chapters show, the iTunes Music Store isn't the only option for downloading tracks from the Internet. But if you use iTunes and an iPod, it's unquestionably the most convenient, offering you instant, legal access to hundreds of thousands of tracks for 79p/99¢ each. Unlike some of its competitors, the iTunes Music Store is not a website, so don't expect to reach it with Internet Explorer or Safari. The only way in is through iTunes: simply connect to the Net, click the Music Store icon in the Source List, and after a few seconds the iTunes window will be taken over by the Store's front page…

music online

What have they got?

At the time of writing, the iTunes Music Store boasts well over two million songs, plus thousands of audiobooks, and claims to have the largest legal download catalogue in the world. However, there are still a lot of glaring omissions, and it isn't like a regular shop where anything can be ordered if you're prepared to wait a while. As with any download site, anything that's up there is the result of a deal struck with the record label in question, and so far, many independent record distributors have refused to sign up. So don't expect to find everything you want.

That said, thousands of new tracks appear week after week, so the situation can only get better. And there are plenty of other places to look if you can't find what you want – see p.151.

Logging in for the first time

Though any iTunes user can browse the Music Store, listen to samples and look at artwork, if you actually want to buy anything you need to set up an account. Which is easily done: hit the Sign In button (top right); press Create New Account (or choose, if you prefer, to use your existing .mac or AOL account details); and follow the prompts to enter your payment and contact details. If someone else is already signed in to the Store on the same computer, they'll need to sign out first.

You'll need your ID and password each time you want to buy something, so keep them safe.

Sign In to buy music on the iTunes Music Store
To create an Apple Account, click Create New Account.

(Create New Account)

If you have an Apple Account (from the Apple Store or .Mac, for example), enter your Apple ID and password. Otherwise, if you are an AOL member, enter your AOL screen name and password.

⦿ 🍎
○ AOL

Apple ID:
Example : steve@mac.com

Password:
(Forgot Password?)

(Cancel) (Sign In)

Apple Store DRM

The songs sold by the Music Store are AAC files protected by DRM (see p.16), which means there are certain encoded restrictions that control what you can actually do with them. At the time of writing, these restrictions are:

▶ The tracks aren't playable on non-Apple software or hardware.

▶ Your downloads can only be "authorized" to play on five computers at any one time. However, you can change which computers these are as often as you need to.

▶ You can burn individual purchased songs to CD as many times as you like, but you can only burn a playlist seven times if it contains purchased songs (you can always recompile the playlist to get around this).

You can get around these restrictions (see p.156), but it's a bit of a hassle.

Navigating

You shouldn't struggle to find your way around the iTunes Music Store. Like online CD stores such as Amazon, it lets you peruse by genre, look at "Staff Favourites", "Featured Artists", "Exclusives" and so on. But it also lets you use the various tools familiar from browsing your own iTunes Library. For example:

Searching

Once you are in the Store the iTunes Search field (see p.54) can be used to search the Store's catalogue. The homepage also features a link to "Power Search" where you can narrow your search criteria.

You can go "up a level", or right back to the Store's homepage, by clicking the tabs at the top right

Browsing

The Browse function works in exactly the same way as it does for your own Library (see p.53): hit the Browse button in the top right corner and then browse genres, artists and albums in the columns that appear.

> TIP: Use the Apple key (Mac) or Ctrl key (Windows) in conjunction with the square-bracket keys to go back and forth between Music Store windows.

Quicklinks

Whether you are browsing your own Library or the Music Store's catalogue, you can use the grey circular Quicklink buttons in the

Song List to quickly access all the Music Store's selections for a particular artist. Quicklinks can be turned on and off for your own Library in iTunes Preferences under General.

> ▶ TIP: Just like any other item in the Source List, double-clicking the Music Store's icon opens it in a separate window.

Previewing music

You can preview thirty seconds' worth of any track within the Music Store catalogue simply by double-clicking the song's name in the Song List. You can also drag any previews into playlists on the Source List to listen to later. These previews will appear in the Song List all ready for you to click when you want to buy the whole track.

> ▶ TIP: If you want to stop your kids either accessing the Music Store entirely or having their tender ears exposed to explicit material, look for the options under the Parental tab of iTunes Preferences.

Buying music

Once you're ready to buy some tracks, there are two ways to go about it. You could use the "1-Click" method, whereby a single click of a Buy Song button in the Song List will debit the payment from your card and start the track downloading to your iTunes Library. Alternatively you can shop using a "Shopping Cart", which appears in the Source List. As you browse the store you add songs to your cart using the Add Song buttons; when you are done, click the cart's icon in the Source List, inspect its contents and then hit the Buy Now button in the bottom right corner to pay and start downloading.

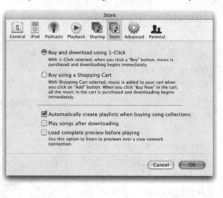

You can set which method you wish to use in the iTunes Preferences panel – look under the Store tab.

> TIP: If you want to quickly see all the music and video you ever purchased from the iTunes Music Store, click "Check for purchases..." in the iTunes Advanced menu.

Authorizing and Deauthorizing

Music purchased from the iTunes Music Store can only be "authorized" for use on five machines at any one time. This way Apple hope that they can curb the unauthorized sharing of copyrighted music. Your computer is authorized to play music you purchase when you set up your account, or when you enter your

ID and password to play a song that you've downloaded.

If your account is already authorized with five computers, you will have to deauthorize one of the machines before playing any of the tracks on a sixth. This is done by selecting Deauthorize computer... from the Advanced menu in iTunes.

If you ever plan to sell or ditch an old machine which has been used to play purchased songs, make sure you deauthorize it before you say goodbye.

> TIP: If you have five computers authorized, you can simultaneously deauthorized them all via the link on your iTunes Music Store account page.

More in the Store

Publish an iMix

As well as selling music, iTunes Store gives you the option of publishing your own playlists so that others can either draw inspiration from (or snigger at) your impeccable taste. Note, though, that

only songs available in the Music Store will be listed.

To publish a playlist, either select it in the Source List and choose Create an iMix... from the File menu, or click the arrow next to its

music online

icon. To email a friend with the link to your published mix, click the arrow button to the right of the published playlist in the Source List and click "Tell a friend".

Giving music

You can buy and send "Gift Certificates" as well as pre-paid "iTunes Music Cards" that can be redeemed in the Store. The link is on the homepage with full instructions. Here you'll also see a link for setting up a "Monthly Gift" allowance account: you authorize someone to spend a set amount of money each month that is then charged to your credit card.

Billboard charts

If you are a patron of the US iTunes Music Store there is also a link on the homepage to the *Billboard* charts, and not just their current listing, but hit parades from years gone by. These can be a useful resource. European shoppers can browse to the US Store via the dropdown menu at the bottom of the homepage.

Freebies

Keep an eye open for free tracks: you get something for nothing, and you might discover an artist you never knew you liked. Also on offer are free-to-stream music videos, though you'll need a fast Internet connection to make them worth watching.

15
More music online

buying music online

Though it's the obvious choice for iTunes users, the iTunes Music Store doesn't hold all the cards when it comes to selling music online. There are many other services out there. Some of them are less expensive than iTunes; others offer tracks that iTunes doesn't; and some even donate their profits to charity. We've covered the full range over the next few pages to give you an idea of what's out there, but, as we explain, many of these aren't immediately compatible with iTunes or the iPod.

151

music online

iPod-compatible services

You can't simply download a song from any site or service and play it back in iTunes and on your Pod. Whether it will work depends on the type of file format that the tracks are saved in, and whether or not the tracks have embedded DRM protection (see p.16).

Unfortunately for iPod owners, the majority of the big online music services (aside from the iTunes Music Store) offer DRM-protected WMA files. Currently, these won't play back in iTunes or on an iPod – at least not without some effort (see box on p.156). And this situation looks unlikely to change any time soon, since Apple are keen to keep people shopping at the iTunes Music Store rather than at any of its competitors.

Realistically, then, for legal music downloads, you're better off sticking with iTunes or the various services that offer unprotected MP3 files. The latter tend to be specialists in independent music, as the smaller labels are more relaxed about allowing their music to be distributed in an unprotected format. These include the following:

Amazon www.amazon.com
Hundreds of free tracks (though not albums, usually). The majority are from up-and-coming artists, though some big names are represented.

AudioLunchbox www.audiolunchbox.com
A top-class selection from independent labels. Most tracks are 99¢, though there are freebies to be had too.

> ▶ The majority of music downloading these days takes place via file-sharing networks. These make it easy and quick to get hold of just about anything you want, for free, but downloading copyrighted music from them is against the law. For more on file sharing, see p.157.

Bleep www.bleep.com
Electronica and indie, including everything from the Warp Records catalogue and loads more. You can preview whole tracks before buying, at which point expect to pay 99p per song or £6.99 for an album.

eMusic www.emusic.com
Perhaps the main competitor to iTunes for iPod owners, this brilliant service offers 600,000 songs from indie labels. For $9.99 per month you get 40 tracks – which works out at only ¢25 per track.

Epitonic www.epitonic.com
Insound www.insound.com/mp3
Freebies from underground and independent artists, mostly from the US.

IntoMusic www.intomusic.co.uk
Indie and alternative stuff for 60p per track. There are subscription and buy-in-bulk payment options for keen users.

Matador Records www.matadorrecords.com
Free offerings from the label whose roster includes Cat Power and Mogwai.

Mperia.com www.mperia.com
A space where unsigned artists can sell, or give away, their music. They keep 70% of anything you pay.

Nervous Records www.nervous.co.uk/download.htm
MP3s from the rockabilly label (not to be confused with its NYC namesake), at 99¢ a shot.

Russian services

In between the legit and the illegit, there are MP3 websites that are, well, kind of legal. All Of MP3, for example, is the best-known of the Russian sites that use a loophole in their country's broadcast law to openly offer a huge download archive without permission from the labels. They offer all formats and bitrate "by the weight" – you buy, say, 100MB for a comparatively tiny fee. It's left up to you to ensure you don't break the law of your own country when downloading.

All Of MP3 www.allofmp3.com

PlayLouder www.playlouder.com
PlayLouder is at present a music site with a decent selection of MP3s at 99p each (£7.99 max for an album). However, look out for this name, as they have recently launched www.playlouderMSP.com, the first legal file sharing network, which could quite easily redefine the way we download music in the future.

Sub Pop Records www.subpop.com
Free tracks from the label who brought us Nirvana and others.

Trax2Burn www.trax2burn.com
House music galore, at 99p per track.

Vitaminic www.vitaminic.com
Unsigned artists of variable quality. Tracks range from free to 99p, with unlimited access at $40 for six months.

Wippit www.wippit.com
Though some of the bigger-name tracks are only available as iPod-unfriendly WMA files, Wippit also offers loads of MP3s – starting at only 29p each. Subscription options also available.

Calabash Music www.calabashmusic.com
World Music served up according to fair-trade principles.

Download.com Music music.download.com
Free music by amateur or up-and-coming artists. It's the archive that used to live at MP3.com – now a site that lets you compare (and search for tracks across) the major music services.

Other services

Aside from the above, the major online music services won't officially work with iTunes, iPods or Macs. Still, PC users might be interested to check them out, perhaps to use them alongside iTunes. (And because, if you're keen enough, it is usually possible to get around the compatibility problem – see box overleaf).

All of the following offer close to – or more than – one million songs. Some are subscription services, some sell individual tracks and others offer both options. When signing up for any subscription service, be sure to read the small print to find out exactly what you're getting for your money. With many "unlimited access" services, for example, you'll find that your downloaded music ceases to play the moment you cancel your subscriptions. With others, the DRM will impose annoying restrictions – such as stopping you burning tracks to CD.

UK services

HMV www.hmv.com
Virgin virgindigital.com
Napster www.napster.com
Three major services offering "permanent" downloads at 79p per song or unlimited access to millions of tracks for £10–15 per month.

OD2 Services www.ondemanddistribution.com
Big Noise Music www.bignoisemusic.com
Founded by Peter Gabriel, OD2 supply the technology and music behind various pay-per-track sites, including those from Ministry Of

Sound, MSN Music, Packard Bell, Tiscali Music Club and Wanadoo. The one that stands out is Big Noise Music, which helps fund Oxfam.

Connect www.connect.com
Sony's pay-per-track download service, available via the same company's "SonicStage" jukebox software, is decent enough, though annoyingly it only works with Sony portable players.

US services

Napster www.napster.com
Rhapsody www.listen.com
Unlimited access to more than 1,000,000 songs for $10 (computer only) or $15 (if you want to use an MP3 player). "Permanent" downloads are separate, at 79–99¢ per track.

BuyMusic www.buymusic.com
Connect www.connect.com
MSN Music music.msn.com
RealPlayer Music Store musicstore.real.com
Virgin www.virgindigital.com
Buy track by track at 79–99¢ per track or around $7.99 per album.

Musicmatch www.musicmatch.com
Unlimited streams, though no proper downloads, for $4.99 per month.

Circumventing the DRM

If you're determined, it is usually possible to get around the iPod-incompatibility of the services listed above. If the DRM on a track doesn't stop you burning it to CD, you could try doing just that and then re-ripping the same track in a non-DRM format. You may also find software online that can strip the DRM protection away, though iTunes 4.7 rendered one of the more popular DRM-strippers useless. There's always the option of playing back the file while re-recording it with an audio editor (see p.136). However, none of these options will do wonders for the sound quality, they may break the terms of your licence agreement, and they're a pain to say the least.

16

P2P file sharing
legalities & practicalities

While the iTunes Music Store may have competition from other commercial download services, it's probably fair to say that its primary competitor is P2P file sharing, a technology that allows computer users all over the world to "share" each other's files – including music files – via the Internet. Even if you've never heard of P2P ("peer-to-peer") you've probably heard of some of the programs that have made this kind of file sharing possible, such as KaZaA and, historically speaking, Napster. And you've probably also heard people debating the legal and moral ins and outs of the free-for-all that file-sharing programs facilitate. If not, don't worry – the next few pages will bring you up to speed.

A peer-to-peer primer

On a home or office network, it's standard for users of each computer to have some degree of access to the files stored on the other computers. P2P file-sharing programs apply this idea to the whole of the Internet – which is, of course, simply a giant network of computers. In short, anyone who installs a P2P program can access the "shared folder" of anyone else running a similar program. And these shared folders are mostly filled with MP3 music files.

With literally millions of file sharers online at any one time, an unthinkably large quantity of music is up there. And it's not just music: any file can be made available, from video and images to software and documents. So, whether you're after a drum'n'bass track, a Web-design application, a Chomsky speech or an episode of *Friends*, you're almost certain to find it. But that doesn't mean that it's legal. If you download or make available any copyright-protected material, you are breaking the law and, while it's still currently unlikely, you could in theory be prosecuted.

The legal battle

Continuous legal action saw Napster – the first major P2P system – bludgeoned into submission (it has now resurfaced as one of the larger legitimate online music providers; see p.155). A similar fate befell Scour, this time because of movie rather than audio sharing. But these casualties just paved the way for the many alternatives, of which the most popular has proved to be KaZaA, which now stands by some margin as the most downloaded program in the history of the Internet.

So far, despite their not inconsiderable efforts, the music, film and software companies have failed to put an end to this new-generation file sharing. Mainly this is because, unlike the old

iP2P?

The market position of iTunes and the iPod is often said to be strengthened by the wide range of third-party software and accessories available for it. But among these are programs that must make Apple – who are eager to get on the right side of the music industry – cringe. It was only a matter of time, for example, before someone developed a program to turn the Mac version of iTunes into a file-sharing program, allowing users around the globe to browse and download from the Libraries of others. That program was iCommune (www.icommune.net), though legal wranglings seem to have stopped it taking the Net by storm.

programs, the new ones create a genuinely decentralized network. In other words, they don't rely on a central system to keep tabs on which files are where. This means that, even though the programs are mostly used for the illegal distribution of copyrighted material, the companies producing them can't easily be implicated in this breach of the law – just as a gun manufacturer couldn't easily be sued for a shooting involving their product.

This immunity wasn't to last, however. In 2005, the Recording Industry Association of America (RIAA) and the Motion Picture Industry (MPI) were successful in closing down the company behind the Grokster P2P program. It remains to be seen how long the others will survive.

In the meantime, the music industry, led by RIAA, has instead gone after the people who clearly *are* breaking the law: individual file sharers downloading or making available copyrighted material. Quite a few individuals have now been prosecuted – in the US, at least – creating a major backlash of public opinion against RIAA. But with many millions of people using file sharing each day, it's inconceivable that the record companies would be able to go after every one of them.

Whether or not it's ethical to use P2P to download copyrighted material for free is another question. Some people justify it on the grounds that they use file sharing as a way to listen to new music they're considering buying on CD; others claim they refuse to support a music industry that, in their view, is doing more harm than good; others still only download non-controversial material, such as recordings of speeches, or music that they already own on CD or vinyl and can't be bothered to rip or record manually.

It's a heated debate – as is the question of whether file sharing has damaged legal music sales, something the industry insists upon, but which many experts claim is questionable. For more on this topic, see p.18.

The networks

Though all P2P file sharing takes place via the Internet, there are various discrete "networks", the main three being **eDonkey2000**, **FastTrack** and **Gnutella**. Each is huge and accessible via various different programs, many of which are very sophisticated, with built-in media players or even the ability to import downloaded tracks directly into a playlist in iTunes.

It's worth noting that some file-sharing programs come with unwelcome extras such as spyware and adware – something long associated with KaZaA, for example. So proceed with care. At a minimum, PC owners should download and regularly run SpyBot S&D (available at www.safer-networking.org). Mac users are much less at risk.

Following is a list of the major networks and some of the popular programs for accessing them. All of these can be downloaded and used for free, though some nag users to make a donation to the developer or pay for a more fully featured or ad-free version. Note that new P2P programs come out all the time, as do upgrades of the existing ones. Also note that some programs can access more than one network – eg Poisoned (Mac) and Shareaza (PC).

Gnutella and Gnutella 2

Gnutella is a very popular network accessible via a wide range of user-friendly programs, including:

Acquisition www.acquisitionx.com (Mac)
LimeWire www.limewire.com (PC & Mac)
Morpheus www.morpheus.com (PC)
Shareaza www.shareaza.com (PC)

FastTrack

Thanks to the success of KaZaA, this extremely well-stocked network has been the focus of much of the legal battle. Other than KaZaA, applications for accessing FastTrack include:

iMesh www.imesh.com (PC)
MLMac www.mlmac.org (Mac)
Poisoned www.gottsilla.net (Mac)

eDonkey2000 & Overnet

The eDonkey2000 network can be accessed via the original eDonkey program, but the newer eMule has more features. The people behind eDonkey also set up the Overnet network, originally intended as

a replacement for eDonkey2000: both now have their own programs, which feed off each other's networks, and both are still growing.

eDonkey2000 www.edonkey2000.com (PC)
eMule www.emule-project.net (PC)
MLDonkey www.nongnu.org/mldonkey (PC & Mac)
Overnet www.overnet.com (PC)

And more…

There are many other programs and networks out there (as well as other ways of sharing files, such as via newsgroups and chat). Soulseek is popular for alternative music and has an active "community", while BitTorrent – with which you start downloads via links on webpages – provides super-fast access to large files, such as complete albums and videos. Find out more at:

SoulSeek www.slsknet.org (PC & Mac)
BitTorrent www.bittorrent.com (PC & Mac)

But don't download just any P2P client or you may end up with spyware in your system. For reviews of all the available programs, plus news and links to download sites, see:

Slyck www.slyck.com (PC & Mac)
ZeroPaid www.zeropaid.com (PC & Mac)
Mac-P2P.com www.mac-p2p.com (Mac)

Legal file sharing

As a final note, PlayLouder MSP is aiming to launch soon as the first file-sharing system specifically setting out to be legally squeaky-clean. The ideal is to combine legal music sharing with broadband in a single package. Many record labels are already on board. Only time will tell if the model proves popular.

PlayLouder MSP www.playloudermsp.com

17

Podcasts & radio

tuning in online

Traditionally, online radio has worked pretty much like radio in the real world, except that the choice of stations is almost endless. You're limited neither by your geographical area nor your next-door neighbour's four-storey gazebo. This is great for listening on your computer, but it can be a hassle, and legally dodgy, to get traditional "streamed" online radio shows onto an iPod. Hence the recent emergence of Podcasts – a new type of online radio aimed specifically at the MP3-player generation. And it's a craze that iTunes has endeavoured to make very much its own. Podcasts are produced by everyone from the BBC to wannabe pundits operating out of their bedrooms. They're easy to make and even easier to find and download.

music online

Podcasts

Unlike most online radio, which is "streamed" across the Net in real time, Podcasts are made available as files (usually MP3s) that can be downloaded and transferred to your iPod or other digital music player. Podcasts are usually free and often consist of spoken content – current affairs, poetry, cookery, etc. There are many musical Podcasts, too, though there's a grey area surrounding the distribution of copyrighted music in this way.

> **TIP:** If you want to stop your kids accessing Podcasts, check the relevant option under the Parental tab of Preferences.

The best way to understand Podcasts is to think of them as "audio blogs". Like regular blogs, they are generally made up of a series of short episodes, or posts; you can subscribe to them via RSS (see box opposite); and they are nearly all free.

Subscribing to Podcasts

It's often possible to download a single Podcast "show" directly from the website of whoever produced it, but it's far easier to use iTunes to subscribe to each of the Podcasts that you're interested in. That way you have fresh news stories, debates, poems, music or whatever each day – ideal for the morning journey to work.

> **TIP:** If you don't get on with iTunes, or you want to get hold of Podcasts for a non-iPod MP3 player, try a third-party Podcast aggregator such as iPodder (ipodder. sourceforge.net) or Life2Go (www.kainjow.com/life2go). Alternatively, visit audio.weblogs.com to browse the most recently posted Podcasts.

Open iTunes and click Podcasts in the Source List. Next, click the Podcast Directory link (at the bottom) and browse or search for interesting-looking Podcasts. When you find one that looks up your street, click subscribe and iTunes will automatically download the most recent episode to your iTunes Library, ready for transfer to your Pod. (Depending on the Podcast, you may also be offered all the previous episodes to download.)

To change how iTunes handles Podcasts, look under the relevant tab in iTunes Preferences. For example, if disk space is at a premium on your system, tell iTunes to delete older episodes after a week or so.

RSS

RSS (**R**eally **S**imple **S**yndication) is the technology behind regular blogs as well as Podcasts (which are basically audio blogs). When you subscribe to a Podcast, your aggregator program (iTunes for example) hooks up with an RSS file, also known as an RSS feed, which is stored online. This file contains information about all the episodes of the Podcast and points iTunes to the relevant sound files. The RSS feed is written in a relatively simple code called XML (it's a bit like the HTML of regular webpages), which makes it quite easy to do yourself (see p.166).

Creating your own Podcast

Once you've subscribed and listened to a few Podcasts you might decide its time to turn your hand to broadcasting and get in on the action. Without going into too much detail, this is how it's done via the iTunes Music Store.

▶ **Record your episode** This can be done pretty easily using a microphone and any of the programs we mention on p.204. When you're finished, save the episode in MP3 or AAC format.

> ▶ TIP: iTunes Podcasting supports various audio (.m4a, .mp3) and video (.mov, .mp4, .m4v) file formats and even .pdf document files. Using a program such as Garageband (see p.137), you can create AAC (.m4a) files that include chapter divisions as well as images that will show up as "album artwork" in both iTunes and on an iPod.

▶ **Create an RSS feed** This is a bit fiddly, but you'll soon get the hang of it. You need nothing more than a text editor, which you'll already have in the form of Notepad (PC) or TextEdit (Mac). For full details on writing your RSS file read the Apple tutorial and sample file at www.apple.com/itunes/podcasts/techspecs.html

▶ **Upload your Podcast** Find or hire some Web space (most Internet connection accounts offer a bit for free), and use an FTP program to upload both the RSS feed and your audio files.

▶ **Test your feed** Make sure you're connected to the Internet and then open iTunes. Choose Subscribe to Podcast... from the Advanced menu and enter the URL (online address) of your RSS feed file. If your Podcast automatically downloads into iTunes, you know that everything is working fine.

▶ **Submit your Podcast to iTunes** From iTunes click the Music Store link in the Source List, then find your way to the store's Podcasts page and click the big "Submit a Podcast" button. Once you've entered the URL of your feed and a few other details, just sit back and wait for an email from Apple telling you that your Podcast has been accepted.

Internet radio

Radio in iTunes

Radio in iTunes is extremely simple.
Connect to the Internet, click the Radio icon in the Source List and browse through the list of genres and stations. For each station you'll see a bitrate – this is important as you will only enjoy a glitch-free listening experience if you select stations which stream at a bitrate that is slower than your Internet connection.

When you've found a station you like the look of, double-click it, wait a few seconds, and the stream should begin. You can create shortcuts to your favourites by dragging them into a playlist.

More Internet radio…

iTunes only scratches the surface of Internet radio. Search Google or browse a directory such as About.com, and you'll find thousands more stations.

About Radio radio.about.com

music online

Most of these stations are accessed via a website. All you need to tune in, if you don't have them already, are the right media players: RealPlayer (there's a free version buried in the site) and Windows Media Player (also free, available for Mac and PC).

RealPlayer www.real.com
Windows Media Player www.windowsmedia.com/download

> ▶ TIP: Programs such as iTunes, Real and WMP "buffer" online radio, delaying the content for a few seconds so that if there's a brief interruption in the stream there's enough in reserve so that you won't notice. If your iTunes radio is prone to glitches, try increasing the Streaming Buffer Size to Large under the Advanced tab in Preferences (see p.45).

…and onto the iPod

There are two main limitations with online radio, apart from the imperfect sound quality. One is that, though some online radio stations offer programmes "on demand", you generally have to be in the right place at the right time to listen to them. Second, you can't access online radio on your iPod. However, there are programs available specifically for getting around these limitations by recording radio onto your hard drive as MP3 files. RadioLover (Mac) and HiDownload (PC), for example, allow you to record shows as MP3s ready to be imported into iTunes. But be aware that, depending on your country, the station, and what you do with the download, recording from a radio stream may not be strictly legal.

HiDownload www.hidownload.com
RadioLover www.bitcartel.com/radiolover

More than music

18

iPod as
hard drive

moving and backing up files

Though they might be revolutionizing the way we listen to music, iPods are, at the end of the day, little more than glorified data storage devices in pretty little boxes. iPods and iPod minis contain a hard drive exactly the same as the one in a computer, while the iPod shuffle and iPod nano use a memory "chip". So it's no surprise that, besides its role as digital music player, an iPod can also function exactly like a standard external drive, storing any type of computer file. Assuming you have some free space on your Pod, you can use it for anything from backing up your photo archive to transporting documents between home and the office. And your Pod will still play music as usual.

more than music

Enabling hard drive use

To use your iPod as a hard drive, first you have to enable this feature. Simply attach the Pod to your computer as usual, and, when iTunes recognizes its presence, click its icon on the Source List and press the iPod Preference button at the bottom of the window (or open the iTunes Preferences window and choose the iPod section). Check the "Enable disk use" box under Music and

don't worry about the "manual unmounting" warning that may pop up – it's only telling you that you'll have to eject the Pod (see p.65) each time you want to disconnect it.

Using the iPod as a hard drive on Mac and PC

When you first plug your iPod into your computer, it prepares it for use by "formatting" the hard drive. iPods formatted on a PC can be recognized by both PCs and Macs, which is great if you're using your iPod as a hard drive, as it means you can move files between nearly all computers. However, iPods formatted on a Mac can only be recognized by Macs. So, if you intend to use your Mac-formatted iPod with both platforms – either to update music manually or to transfer files – consider reformatting the Pod on a PC. This should only be done using the iPod Software Updater program, which will have come on a CD with the Pod. Before running the program, try checking the Apple website (see p.246) to see if a more up-to-date version is available to download. Then set it running and choose Restore (not Update). Note that this will delete all music, contacts and notes that the Pod contains – you'll have to move everything back onto it afterwards.

iPod shuffle disk use

One of the best things about the iPod shuffle is the fact that its size makes it the perfect device for transporting work between home and the office without having to worry about docks and cables in both locations. All very well, but it's not much use if it's stuffed to the gills with music. The solution can be found within the iPod Preferences pane – when enabling disk use for an iPod shuffle you are also offered a slider that lets you determine how much of your shuffle you want to leave free each time the music is updated.

> ☑ Enable disk use
>
> Choose how much space will be reserved for songs versus data.
>
> 120 Songs ○━━━━━━━━━━━━━━ 0 MB Data
>
> More Songs   More Data

> **TIP:** Compared to other models the iPod shuffle is not a particularly capacious beast. However, if you are so inclined, you could combine the capacity of several shuffles to create a RAID-style "shuffle array". Here's where to find out how: ipod.hackaday.com

Using your new drive

Once disk use has been enabled, your iPod will appear as a standard drive (or volume), as well as within iTunes, whenever you connect it to your computer. On a Mac it appears on the Desktop and in the left-hand column of Finder windows (as shown overleaf); in this state, the drive is said to be "mounted". On a PC it appears within My Computer as an external drive icon with a drive identification letter (perhaps "F:" or "G:").

Now you can use the drive as you would any other volume

within either Windows or Mac OS: view its contents (though your music will be invisible), create folders, drag files on, drag files off. And so on.

You'll probably find several folders in the iPod's drive when you open it: these relate to iPod organizer functions (see p.191) and photo functions (see p.175). None of these folders should be deleted.

Ejecting your drive

When you are done with the drive, eject it (or "dismount" it) in the same way you would whenever the "Do not disconnect" message is displaying (see p.65).

One for Mac spods – the iPod startup disk

Do you own an iBook or PowerBook? Are you technically minded? Then you could try installing the recovery software that came with your Mac onto your iPod. This would give you a useful means of restarting and repairing your computer if it ever died when you were out and about and you didn't have the CDs to hand. You can even go the whole way and install a fully working OS to your Pod, though it may never play music again. Both these activities are beyond the scope of this book, but if you fancy giving them a go, look online for tips and advice. For a list of relevant websites, see p.247.

iPods & photos

pictures in your pocket

As we've just seen, iPods can be used as hard drives to store all types of files. This includes digital photos, which can be manually dragged onto any Pod (or automatically backed up there with a program such as Life2Go, see p.224). This is fine for showing off your snaps on other people's computers, but with a colour-screen iPod model you can also display photos on your Pod's screen. This chapter provides a quick photo tutorial.

more than music

iPod as photo album

The iPod isn't going to revolutionize photography in the same way it and other MP3 players have changed the way we listen to music. That said, the colour-screen models are a very nifty step up in terms of the gadget's evolution, allowing you to get your computer's existing library of digital images into your pocket in a form that can be viewed both on the Pod's own screen or via a TV.

Putting pics onto your iPod

Whether you use a Mac or PC, it's iTunes (version 4.7 or higher) that handles the task of moving pictures from your computer to your iPod. It can move images over from any standard folders – such as the My Pictures folder in Windows, or the Pictures folder in OS X – but it's better to use iTunes in conjuction with a program that lets you arrange your photos into albums. At the time of writing, only a handful of programs are supported:

iPhoto (Mac) www.apple.com/iphoto (bundled with all new Macs)
Photoshop Album (PC) www.adobe.com/photoshopalbum ($50/£40)
Photoshop Elements (Mac/PC) www.adobe.com/photoshopelements ($90/£60)

To get things started, connect your iPod to your computer and open the iTunes Preferences window. In the iPod pane, choose Photos, tick the box that enables synchronization and then choose the source of your photos from the dropdown menu. The My Pictures and Pictures folders will appear in this list by default on PC and Mac respectively, as will any compatible photo-manage-

> TIP: iPods supports JPEGs, BMPs, GIFs, TIFFs and PNGs.
> If a photo doesn't display, make sure it's in one of these formats. If not, resave it.

ment programs installed on your system (if your images are elsewhere use the Choose Folder option to browse for them). At the bottom of the window you will see a running total of how many pics you have selected to sync.

During the sync process iTunes creates two resized, space-efficient versions of your originals for displaying on the screen and, if you have a standard iPod, a third for displaying on a TV (the iPod nano does not support TV photo viewing). Check the box at the bottom of the photo preferences window if you additionally want to copy the higher-quality originals to your iPod, so that you can print them or pass them on to friends and family when away from home. They can then be accessed from the Photos folder in a sub-folder labelled Full Resolution when your iPod is being used in disk mode (see p.171).

When you are done, click OK and the photos will wing their way onto your Pod. Be patient, this can take a while…

View images on your iPod

Once your images are on the iPod, photo navigation is intuitive and requires little elaboration. Choose Photo from the top level menu and then browse the albums and images just as you would songs, using the select button to view a specific image and the skip forward and back buttons to do just that.

To kickstart a slideshow, use the ▶︎❙❙ button (if you have an album or thumbnail selected) or the Select button (if you're already viewing a single image). For playback options, explore the Slideshow Settings (at the top of the Photo menu). Here you can add music to a slideshow, shuffle the images and turn on *Star Wars*-esque

more than music

transitions between photos. Also use this menu to enable the TV-out signal (sorry – not for nano owners) and specify whether your TV requires NTSC (US) or Pal (Europe) signals.

Connecting to a TV

Standard colour-screen iPods can be connected to TVs via either AV or S-video cables, both available separately. AV is the less expensive option, and will work with nearly all modern TVs: a minijack plug connects directly to the Pod, and three colour-coded plugs (red and white for sound, yellow for pictures) connect to the TV. S-video cables provide better picture quality, but they cost more and can only be used with a Dock (see p.208).

Note that iPods struggle to display very large slideshows via a TV, so try to avoid albums that contain more than around 200 images.

What else?

That's pretty much it, but the possibilities are only really limited by your imagination. You could, for example, export PowerPoint presentations as JPEGs and run them from your Pod. The application iPresent It makes this easy on a Mac:

iPresent It www.zapptek.com

Or create flipbook-style animations by scrolling through albums of specially prepared images. You could even buy two iPods and spend the weekend constructing a stereoscope…

20

iPods & video

How to download or roll your own

All iPods can store video files (see p.181) but only the latest full-size model – the fifth generation iPod – can actually play them back. It's a feature that was eagerly anticipated for years before finally arriving in October 2005. With such small screens, video iPods pose no threat to televisions, but being able to play music videos, home movies and even DVDs on your Pod is occasionally useful – and often fun.

more than music

Stocking up on videos

Just as with music, before you can transfer videos to your iPod, you first have to get them into iTunes. There are a few options: downloading ready-made iPod-compatible videos, or creating your own from existing video files, DVDs or TV. Let's look at each in turn…

Downloading videos from iTunes

When Apple launched the video iPod, much fanfare was made about the fact that the iTunes Music Store (see p.143) would start selling music videos, a few Pixar animations, and – in the US only – TV shows such as *Lost* and *The Office*, plus a bunch of oddities from the Disney empire. This is now an integral part of the Store, with thousands of music videos available already and more being added every day.

Perhaps more interesting than this content (most of which can be watched for free, in much higher quality, on television) is the growing number of video Podcasts to be found within the iTunes Podcast Directory (see p.165). Ranging from the comedic (*The Ricky Gervais Podcast*) to the didactic (*Learn Excel with MrExcel*), video Podcasts offer much more digestible, journey-to-work-sized chunks of video, and they're free to boot.

> ▶ TIP: To search for music videos in the iTunes Store, enter an artist's name in the search field and then click the Video button that appears on the search bar.

Downloading videos from iTunes works in just the same way as with music (see p.148). After you've downloaded a video file, it will be deposited in your general iTunes Library, though all your

Video formats

Video files are more confusing than most, as you have to worry not only about the file format (which you can usually tell by the file extension: eg .mov and .avi) but also the "codec" (compression technique) used to create the file. To make things even more complex, various other factors – such as frames per second and audio formats – may also affect whether a particular file can play back on a particular piece of hardware or software.

In short, video-capable iPods support files in the .m4v, .mp4 and .mov formats created using H.264 and MPEG-4 codecs. In full, the supported video specifications are as follows:

▶ **H.264 video** up to 768 Kbps, 320 x 240, 30 frames per second, Baseline Profile up to Level 1.3 with AAC-LC up to 160 Kbps, 48 kHz, stereo audio in file formats.

▶ **MPEG-4 video** up to 2.5 Mbps, 480 x 480, 30 frames per second, Simple Profile with AAC-LC up to 160 Kbps, 48 kHz, stereo audio in .m4v, .mp4 and .mov file formats.

video files can be viewed together by clicking the Video icon in the Source List. For more on playing and transferring your iTunes videos, see p.188.

Importing existing video files

If you have some video files on your computer and you want to get them onto your Pod, you first need to convert them to an iPod-compatible format. In most cases (with MOV, MPEG and MP4 files) this is as simple as dragging the file into your iTunes library, highlighting them in the Song List and then selecting "Convert Selection for iPod" from the iTunes

more than music

Advanced menu. Once that's done, you can delete the older file from iTunes (check the Date Added column in the Song List to be sure which is which). Next time you update your iPod, the video should transfer across.

With certain video files, however, you may find that this approach doesn't work. In these cases, you need to grab some extra software to help you convert the files to the necessary format:

▶ **QuickTime Pro** www.apple.com/quicktime/pro (PC and Mac)
QuickTime Pro, which costs $30/£20, is the advanced version of Apple's free media player and can handle most video file types (though not Windows Media Player). Once you have your video file open in QuickTime, simply press Export in the File menu and choose the "Movie to iPod (320x240)" option. Take the resulting file and drag it onto the Library icon in iTunes.

▶ **Video2Go** www.onlymac.de/indexe.html (Mac only)
This $10 application is even simpler than QuickTime Pro. It lets you browse for video files already on your Mac, then handles the conversion and drops the converted files straight into your iTunes library.

▶ **ffmpegX** homepage.mac.com/major4 (Mac only)
This intimidatingly named tool (which is free to download and use but requests a $15 fee from those who like and use it) gives

> **TIP:** Mac owners can export iPod-ready versions of their home movies from iMovie HD via the Share option in the File menu. Click the QuickTime button and choose Expert Settings, then "Movie to iPod (320x240)".

complete control over various file format settings. However, to get it working you'll need to install a couple of other free files, and to mess about a bit with a few settings. For a clear tutorial, see: arstechnica.com/guides/tweaks/ipod-video.ars/3

Importing DVDs

In most cases, it's perfectly possible to get DVDs onto your iPod, though in some countries this may not be strictly legal when it comes to copyrighted movies. The process depends on your computer.

On a Mac

If you have a Mac, getting a DVD into an iPod-compatible version is a cinch, thanks to a great little free application called HandBrake. Be warned, however, that the process can take a couple of hours to complete once you've set it going. Follow these steps:

▶ **Download HandBrake** from www.handbrake.com and install it by dragging the file named HandBrake into your Applications folder. (If the download provides two folders with different numbers, use the higher numbered version.)

▶ **Insert the DVD** and, if it starts to play automatically, press Apple+Q to exit the player.

---

more than music

▶ **Launch HandBrake** and it should detect the DVD (it will call it something unfriendly like "/dev/rdisk1"). Press Open, and wait until the application has scanned the DVD.

▶ **Plug in the three magic settings...**

1. Set Codecs to: MPEG-4 Video / AAC Audio

2. Set Average bitrate (kbps) to 750

3. Click the Picture settings... button and lower the width to 320. Then, close the Picture settings window.

▶ **Check the source** It's also worth taking a quick look at the "Title" dropdown menu within the Source section of HandBrake. If the list offers several options, choose the one that seems to represent the largest amount of time (for example 01h22m46s) as this

Recording from TV

If you want to be able to record from TV to iPod, you'll need a TV receiver for your computer. Some posh PCs have these built in, but if yours doesn't you should be able to pick one up relatively inexpensively, and attach it to your PC or Mac via USB or FireWire.

As usual, things are easiest for Mac users, thanks to Elgato's superb EyeTV range of portable TV receivers, some of which are as small as an iPod. With an EyeTV, it's easy to record TV shows and then export them directly into an iPod-friendly format. For more info, see:

Elgato www.elgato.com

PC users have many brands of TV receiver/recorders available, though at the time of writing none allows you to export directly in an iPod-friendly format. Instead, record the shows in any format of your choice and use QuickTime Pro to resave them for the iPod.

> **TIP: If your home-recorded iPod videos display horizontal lines during playback, try locating and enabling a "deinterlace" option in whichever program you're using to save them into an iPod-friendly format.**

185

more than music

> **TIP:** If you check the "2-pass encoding" box, this will double the time it takes to process your movie, but the quality will be better, and with no increase in the size of the final file.

should be the main feature. If nothing appears of an appropriate length, then your DVD is copy protected (see box below).

▶ **Rip** Hit the Rip button at the bottom of the window and put your feet up while your Mac does all the hard work. This can take quite a while.

▶ **Drop the file into iTunes** Unless you chose to save it somewhere else, the file will eventually appear on the Desktop. It will probably be in the region of a few hundred megabytes, depending on the length of the DVD. Drag the file onto the iTunes Library icon.

DVD copy protection

DVDs are often encrypted, or copy protected, to stop people making copies or ripping the discs to their computers. PC owners can use a program such as AnyDVD (www.slysoft.com) to get around the protection, while Mac owners trying to get encrypted DVDs onto their iPods will need to grab a program such as Fast DVD Copy (www.fastdvdcopy.com). This allows you to make a non-protected copy, which you can then get onto your iPod in the standard way. For more on this process, and other applications that do the job, see *The Rough Guide to Macs & OS X*. Note that, in some countries, it may not be legal to copy an encrypted DVD.

On a PC

There are various easy-to-use PC applications for getting a DVD onto an iPod, plus a few more in the pipeline (including a Windows version of HandBrake). Of those available at the time of writing, the pick of the bunch is ImTOO DVD to iPod Converter. This DVD-ripping software will convert your movies to iPod video MP4 format and can also handle various audio formats. Among other features, the application allows you to choose between audio tracks on the DVD and, if your eyes are up to it, add subtitles to your final iPod-ready video file.

ImTOO www.imtoo.com/dvd-to-ipod-converter.html $29

For a few dollars more you could try out Xilisoft's DVD to iPod Suite, which guides you through the process in simple step-by-step style.

Xilisoft DVD to iPod Suite www.xilisoft.com

more than music

Playing videos in iTunes

Whether they've been downloaded or imported, all videos in your iTunes Library are gathered together under the Videos icon in the Source List. They can also be found when the Library icon is highlighted, either in the main list, along with all your songs, or by searching and then pressing the Video button in the search bar.

When you double-click a video it will start to play in the little panel, bottom-left. Click this thumbnail version and the video will appear in a separate window. Alternatively, click the last of the five buttons arranged along the bottom-left of the iTunes window to view the video in full-screen mode.

Any videos you import (rather than download from iTunes) will be classified as a "movie" – even if it's actually a music video

Click here to switch between list and thumbnail view

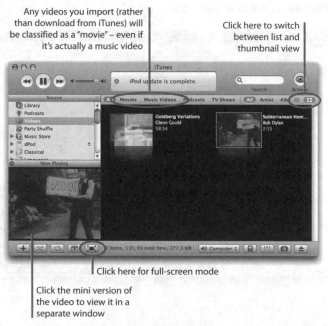

Click here for full-screen mode

Click the mini version of the video to view it in a separate window

> ▶ TIP: Just as with music (see p.70), videos can be
> assembled into playlists in iTunes. You can combine
> videos and movies with songs or keep them separate.
> Note that Smart Playlists (see p.71) will automatically include
> videos that meet their criteria unless you specify otherwise.

As with music, you can easily edit the name, artist or other tags for each of your music videos and movies. Either click directly into a field in the Song List, or select one or more videos and press Apple+I (Mac) or Control+I (PC).

Videos on the iPod

Unless you specify otherwise, all the videos that you've assembled in iTunes will be automatically copied across to your video-capable iPod each time you connect it to your computer. This is fine in most cases, but if you want to save space on your Pod, or if you've amassed a huge collection of feature-length movies within iTunes, you might prefer to be selective about which video files you do and don't upload to your Pod.

Uploading selectively

The easiest option is to create a new playlist (see p.70), name it something like "Videos for iPod", and keep it full of whichever videos you want on your Pod at any one time. If you're so inclined, you could even set up a Smart Playlist (see p.71) to gather together, say, your ten most recently added videos.

Next, connect your Pod, open iTunes Preferences and click the iPod button at the top. Under the Video tab, choose the "Automatically update selective playlists only" option and select the relevant playlist.

In the same panel, you'll find an option for stopping any videos uploading to your Pod.

On the Pod

Once you've uploaded your videos to your iPod, you'll find them via the top-level menu. As with music, hit the central button to choose a video, and then scroll to change the volume. To fast-forward or rewind, press the central button while a video is playing and then use the scroll wheel to move to a different point.

▶ iPod
Music
Photos
Videos
Extras

Playing iPod videos through a TV

As with photos, it's possible to play the videos on your iPod via a TV, though don't expect amazing picture quality, as videos formatted for use on an iPod are only a few hundred pixels across. To connect the iPod to the TV, you could purchase an iPod AV cable ($19/£15), but it's less expensive to buy a generic cable with standard yellow/red/white RCA connectors at one end and a three-banded minijack at the other. These look very similar to Apple's AV cable, but will only work with an iPod if you shuffle the colours around when you connect to the TV:

AV cable white ▶ TV jack red
AV cable red ▶ TV jack yellow
AV cable yellow ▶ TV jack white

To minimize quality loss you could instead use an S-video cable attached to your iPod via an Apple iPod Universal Dock (see p.208).

Once your iPod is hooked up, select Videos in the main menu, hit Video Settings, and turn TV Out on.

21

iPod as organizer

contacts, dates, email and wake-up calls

As a record collection in your pocket, the iPod is superb. As a portable hard drive, it's equally excellent. As an organizer, it's a bit more basic, and doesn't offer anything like the range of features of a proper PDA. Still, the functions it does have are certainly useful. It can act as an address book, taking the contacts database from your computer's address book. It can display a calendar of appointments, or your unread emails (albeit in plain-text format). And it can even wake you up in the morning with a playlist of your choice.

Contacts, calendars and emails

more than music

Getting contacts onto your iPod from your computer – or even from a mobile phone – is not too difficult, assuming that you can export the contacts info, from wherever it currently lives, in the vCard format. Once you've done that, it's simply a matter of putting the vCards into the Contacts folder, which you'll find inside your iPod if you enable it as a hard drive (see p.172). Calendars, similarly, need to find their way into the iPod's Calendars folder in either the iCalendar or vCalendar format. Finally, emails need to become plain-text documents and be put into your iPod's Notes folder (see p.196).

You can do all this manually by exporting the data from the relevant program and saving it onto the iPod, but it's far easier to use iTunes or some other syncing program. That way you don't need to worry too much about file formats and you know the contacts, mail and appointments on the Pod will always be kept up to date. Here's a brief look at how you might sync things from some common programs:

▶ **Address Book, iCal & Mail (Mac)**
Open iPod Preferences (see
p.58) and choose how you'd like
things to work in the Contacts
or Calendars tabs. Job done. If
you also want to transfer your
email, check out a program such
as Life2Go (see p.224), or – if
you have the Mac OS X v10.4
operating system ("Tiger")
– explore the Example Workflows
in Automator, which you'll find
in the Applications folder.

▶ **Outlook & Outlook Express (PC)**
iTunes can automatically transfer
Outlook contacts and calendars,
and Outlook Express contacts,
to an iPod. This is easy to set up
under the relevant tabs of iPod
Preferences (see p.58). If you also
want to transfer Outlook emails,
tasks and notes, however, try downloading the demo versions of:

iPodSync www.ipod-sync.com
Pocket Mac (PC Edition) www.pocketmac.net

▶ **Microsoft Entourage (Mac)** Your best bet is to use the Mac version
of Pocket Mac, which will transform your contacts, calendars,
tasks, notes and emails into an iPod-friendly format.

Pocket Mac www.pocketmac.net

▶ **Palm Desktop (Mac and PC)** It's easy to get your contacts from
your Palm onto your iPod. On a Mac, use iSync (which you'll
find in the Applications folder) to get the information into your
Mac's address book, and then use iTunes to transfer them, as
described opposite. On a PC, try the Palm2iPod plug-in:

Palm2iPod maxnoy.com/ipod

...and on the iPod

Once all this information is safely aboard your Pod, browsing it
is easy: select Extras and then Contacts, Calendars or (for emails)
Notes. If you use these options a lot, you might want to put them
in the top-level menu, which you can do by selecting Settings,
then Main Menu.

more than music

In the Calendars menu you can set an alarm – either a beep or an on-screen text message – to alert you to any appointments to which an alarm setting has been assigned in the mother program. The Calendars menu also offers access to the To Do menu, where tasks that have travelled over from your Mac or PC are stored.

> TIP: You can use the ◀◀ and ▶▶ buttons on your iPod to skip back and forth between appointments within calendars.

iPod clock and alarm clock

Select Clock from the iPod's Extras menu and you'll be presented with a handy little timepiece that also has an alarm feature. You can set the date, time and alarm time by selecting Date & Time from the Settings menu.

Here you can also choose whether you'd like to display the clock at the top of the iPod screen and, if you're using the alarm clock, how you'd like it to sound. The beep is audible, but only lasts for a few seconds, so don't rely on it to get you up in time for a job interview. Alternatively, you can choose to be woken by a playlist of your choice but, unless you like to sleep wearing a pair of headphones, this will rely on you having your iPod hooked up to a stereo (see p.129) or a pair of external speakers (see pp.214–215). When the alarm is set a small bell appears on the right of the screen.

If you want to be woken up by music when travelling, consider a unit such as Griffin's iTalk (see p.204).

> TIP: If you want to use your computer as a musical alarm clock, download an iTunes controller with alarm clock features (see p.223).

22
Notes, news & books

the iPod reader

One of the most useful non-music features of the iPod are "notes", which allow you to read text documents – anything from news stories and travel directions to essay drafts – when you're out and about. You can make your own notes, download them from the Web or even have a program automatically add up-to-date newsfeeds to your Pod each time you plug it in. Various full-length books are on offer as notes and other iPod screen-based formats, such as so-called PodScrolls, and thousands more are available as spoken-word audio recordings. Read on…

more than music

Notes

Also known as PodBooks, notes are simple-text files (text documents with no formatting) that reside within a special folder on your iPod's hard drive. To access this folder, you may first need to enable your iPod for disk use (see p.172). Then open the iPod drive in Windows or Mac OS X and locate the Notes folder.

Any simple-text doc placed in here can be read on the Pod by navigating to the Notes menu in Extras (you can also add it to the top-level menu, by heading for the Settings menu and activating it under Main Menu). To delete text docs from your iPod, simply drag the files from the Notes folder to the Trash (Mac) or Recycle Bin (PC). Or, to keep them on the Pod but stop them displaying, move them out of the Notes folder to anywhere else on the Pod's hard drive. At the time of writing, the Notes folder can handle up to 1000 documents.

Creating your own notes

All word processors can create and re-save docs in simple text (or "text only") format. But don't save over your original file, as the plain-text version will strip out all formatting, such as colours, fonts and underlining. And note that if the resulting file is any bigger than 4KB (roughly 4000 characters), you'll have to chop it up into smaller chunks in order to make it readable on the iPod.

Obviously, you can copy text from webpages or elsewhere, paste it into a word processor and save the result as a text-only doc. But there are also programs that will create Pod-readable text files automatically. iPodLibrary, for example, will convert eBooks in either the .pdf or .lit formats into "notes":

iPodLibrary sturm.net.nz (PC only)

Though few people bother, it is possible to include links within your notes. When clicked, a link can kick-start an audio track, display a photo or open another note. This is done with HTML, the code used to create webpages (unfortunately, the iPod's HTML abilities don't go much beyond links, so don't expect any formatting options). It's even possible to put the iPod into "NotesOnly" or "Museum" mode, which temporarily locks all other iPod functions. The aim is to allow museums and galleries to use iPods for audio tours triggered via notes, but the same function can also be a fun way to leave a message for someone on their iPod. For full details on all these advanced notes functions visit:

Macworld www.macworld.com/2004/09/secrets/septgeekfactor

iSpeak

If you have a Mac, and fancy having notes read out to you, turn to iSpeak It, which can turn written documents into spoken-word AAC files and inject them into your iTunes Library. It also features links to convert Google News, weather forecasts and the text from any webpage into a similar speech file, all ready for you to take out and about on your Pod. However, the program uses the computerized voice that you might have heard barking at you when an error message appears on screen – so don't expect a sympathetic interpretation of your favourite William Blake poem.

Fonix iSpeak can create spoken-word files for PC users, though it lacks the neat iTunes integration.

iSpeak It www.zapptek.com/ispeak-it
Fonix iSpeak www.fonix.com

Downloading notes

Shall I compare thee to Apple's flagship hard-disk-based MP3 music player? Take a look online and you'll find iPod-friendly versions of everything from the best of the Bard to healthfood recipes. Start here:

The American Constitution www.acslaw.org/misc/iPoddl.htm
Formula 1 Encyclopedia www.kimistuff.com/ipod.html
iPodBadger www.ipodbadger.com
Shakespeare Sonnets www.westering.com/ipod
Vegan recipes www.enriquequinterodesign.com

And for a list of note-based games, jokes, chat-up lines and trivia quizzes on everything from *The Simpsons* to *Lord Of The Rings*, visit:

iPod Arcade ipodarcade.com

Newsfeeds

There are now several applications that will convert RSS feeds into notes form. This can be great for keeping up to date with news, blogs and other websites. Life2Go and iPodSync (see p.224 for more on both) can handle RSS (see p.165), though often you'll only get a headline and one-sentence summary for each article, so you might prefer iPDA (www.zapptek.com/iPDA), which pulls whole stories from Google News.

more than music

PodScrolls & maps

The problem with notes is that they can't include images – nor formatting such as fonts, colours and bold text. So-called PodScrolls get around this problem by exploiting the photo capabilities of all colour-screen iPods. PodScrolls are in full colour, with page numbers, images and more – just like real books, but much quicker to flick through. Rough Guides have been the first company to exploit this new format, offering eating and drinking guides to ten of the world's great cities.

Rough Guides PodScrolls www.roughguides.com/podscrolls

In a similar vein, iSubwayMaps produce full-colour metro maps for cities around the world. Like PodScrolls, they are accessed via the iPod's Photos menu.

iSubwayMaps www.isubwaymaps.com

iSubwayMaps.com
download maps | faq | about this site | contact

Berlin, Germany
Bilbao, Spain
Boston, MA
Chicago, IL
Hong Kong
London, UK
Los Angeles, CA
Lyon, France
Melbourne, Australia
Milan, Italy

Paris, France
Philadelphia, PA
Salt Lake City
San Diego, CA
San Francisco, CA
Seoul, Korea
Singapore
Tokyo, Japan
Toronto, ON
Vancouver, BC

Audiobooks

When it comes to spoken-word content, the most obvious point of call for iPod owners is the audiobook section of the iTunes Music Store. It offers thousands of titles – from language primers to classic recordings of great novels made by famous actors – and works in just the same way as the rest of the Store (see p.143).

Also worth exploring is Audible. It has a bigger range than iTunes (27,000 titles at the time of writing) and offers various membership plans that can work out as good value for regular audiobook purchasers.

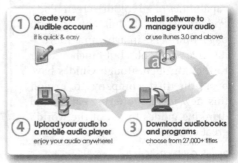

1. Create your Audible account — it is quick & easy
2. Install software to manage your audio — or use itunes 3.0 and above
4. Upload your audio to a mobile audio player — enjoy your audio anywhere!
3. Download audiobooks and programs — choose from 27,000+ titles

Audible www.audible.com

> TIP: Audiobooks from Audible and iTunes are stored in the Audible format (.aa). This means that when you press stop or pause while listening on your iPod or computer, a "bookmark" will be added at that point. When you return to the audiobook, it will start where you left off.

Not that audiobooks necessarily have to cost anything at all. Search online and you'll come across thousands of freebies, served up by sites such as:

Audiobooks For Free www.audiobooksforfree.com
Telltale Weekly www.telltaleweekly.org

Extras

23

Accessories

plug and play

There are scores of iPod accessories available, from the obvious – cases of all shapes and sizes – to the less obvious, such as digital-camera card readers. The following pages show some of the most useful and desirable add-ons out there, but new ones come out all the time, so keep an eye on iPod news sites (see p.246). When it comes to purchasing, some accessories can be bought on the high street, but for the best selection and prices look online. Compare the offerings of the Apple Store, Amazon, eBay and others, or go straight to the manufacturers, many of which sell direct. Before buying any accessory, make sure it is compatible with the iPod model you own.

extras

Voice recorders

Models include: Belkin Voice Recorder; Griffin iTalk; Belkin Universal Microphone Adapter
Cost (approx): $30–50/£25–40

Journalists, writers and thinkers who want to be able to record interviews or thoughts on the move will welcome the opportunity to turn their iPod into a Dictaphone capable of recording hundreds – even thousands – of hours of audio. Voice recorders let you do just this. They plug into the headphone jack, and usually also the remote-control connector, offering a built-in microphone and often a socket for an external mic as well.

Some models lack a headphone jack, but a built-in speaker means that you don't have to unplug the device to hear what you've recorded. Once you're done, the sounds are saved as mono WAV files, ready for transfer to a computer for storage, compressing, emailing or editing. No software or drivers are typically required, so you can literally just plug in and start talking.

If you want more control over the recording level, get the Belkin Universal Microphone Adapter, which has a variable gain switch. But don't expect perfect sound: Apple have deliberately capped the iPod's recording abilities, presumably to stop people bootlegging concerts.

A voice recorder with a speaker also allows you to use your iPod as a portable musical alarm clock – see p.194

Battery packs

Models include: Belkin Backup Battery Pack; Belkin TunePower Rechargable
Cost (approx): $60/£40

If you don't find the iPod's battery lasts long enough, an external battery pack will allow you to keep the music playing for longer. The Belkin model pictured attaches to the Pod with non-scratch suction cups and takes four standard AA batteries (enough for around fifteen to twenty hours of extra playing time).

Battery packs do exactly what they say on the tin, but if you mainly use your iPod in the car, you'll get better value from an in-car power cable (see p.211).

Or, if you don't mind kissing goodbye to your warranty, check out the following page about making your own battery pack from a playing-card box, a FireWire socket, and a few other bits and bobs you probably don't have lying around:
drewperry.co.uk/
index.php?do=iPod&ipod=battery

extras

FM radio transmitters

Models include: Belkin TuneCast; Griffin iTrip; XtremeMac AirPlay
Cost (approx): $40–60 (not available in the UK)

These cunning little devices turn an iPod into an extremely short-range FM radio station (many of them will also work with a computer or any other device with a headphone jack, though check before buying). Once you've attached a transmitter to your iPod, any radio within range (theoretically around 30 feet, though a few feet is more realistic to achieve decent sound) can then tune in to whatever the Pod is playing. The sound quality isn't quite as good as you'd get by attaching to a stereo via a cable (see p.130) and there can be interference, especially in cities. But they are very convenient and allow you to play through any FM radio, including those – such as portables and car stereos – which don't offer a line-in.

Of the models available at the time of writing, the iTrip (pictured; available in black or white) has the advantage of taking power directly from the Pod, so no batteries are required and there are no annoying cables. However, some users have complained of a weak signal compared to other models such as the Belkin TuneCast (which takes two AAA batteries or plugs into the mains or a car socket).

FM transmitters are currently legal in North America but not in the UK, where they breach radio transmission laws. This doesn't seem to have stopped many Brits importing them from the States.

Cables & connections

TV connection cables

Models include: The Monster iTV Link; Apple iPod AV Cable
Cost (approx): $20–$40/£15–£30

If you want to connect your colour-screen
iPod to a TV, you'll need either an AV
cable or an S-video cable. Apple do
a very "white" AV cable, though
a regular AV to three-striped
minijack will do (see p.130).
To go the S-video route
you'll need the appro-
priate Apple Dock (see
p.208) and a cable similar
to the Monster iTV Link
(pictured).

Headphone splitters

Models include: splitters by Monster and others
Cost (approx): $10/£5

Headphone splitters allow you to
connect two pairs of headphones
to a single iPod (or any other
personal stereo).

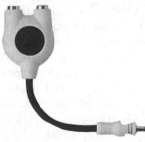

extras

Docks & stands

Models include: Apple iPod Dock; Decodock
Cost (approx): $15–40/£10–30

An iPod "dock" makes it easy to connect and disconnect your Pod to computers, power sources, hi-fis and TVs. The Dock's various connections can be left permanently in place, so when you get home you simply drop your Pod and it's instantly hooked up.

Apple's own Universal Dock features a genuine line-out socket – as opposed to a headphone socket – so the sound quality is improved when playing through a hi-fi. It also boasts an infrared receiver for the Apple Remote (see p.218) and ports for using an AV or S-video cable to view photos or videos on a connected TV.

For a while, Apple shipped all high-end iPods with a Dock, but currently you have to buy one separately. Apple's Universal Dock is pricey, but comes with adapters for several iPod models (check the Apple website to see that your model is covered before you buy). Third-party equivalents tend to be less expensive but aren't all well made. Whichever brand you choose, be sure to get the right dock for your specific iPod model.

Docks come in all shapes and sizes – with price tags to match. Perhaps you'd like something nice in walnut or maple (see www.westshorecraftworks.com). Or if you fancy cobbling your iPod, Flintstones style, pick up an i-Stone (www.brand-incubator.com). A snip at $2650.

01 about us
02 our branding
03 our works
04 e-consulting
05 awards
06 partners
07 new products

07 New Products

BRAND INCUBATOR. Ltd.

i-Stones sabi

石狩平野に聳える
ビンネシリ山。
そのふもとから出土した
「木石」と
「iPod カラー用Dog」の融合作。

_USB 2.0 With Computer
_Battery charging
_Audio connector
_S-video connector
_2-Year Warranty
_2.6Kg

◤back ◥next

Early Pods (first and second generation) don't have a Dock Connector on the bottom, so the only equivalent products available – such as the BookEndz iPodDock – hold your iPod upside down, making the controls hard to use. If you'd rather have your Pod the right way up, you could opt for a simple stand instead, such as Bubble Design's Habitat.

Architecturally minded iPod shuffle owners, meanwhile, should look no further than the splendid, luminous Decodock, available from pressuredropinc.com.

extras

Digital camera accessories

Models include: **Apple iPod Camera Connector; Belkin Media Reader & Digital Camera Link**
Cost (approx): $30–90/£20–70

Most digital cameras store pictures on a tiny removable card. These tend to have a relatively small capacity of, say, 64 or 128 megabytes – plenty for most users, but not enough for serious photographers who want to take a large number of high-quality images without having to return home to their computer to download them. One option is to buy extra cards, but these are quite expensive for the storage capacity they provide. Another option is to use an iPod (which has incomparably higher capacity) as a temporary home for your pictures.

If you have a standard colour-screen iPod, all you need is Apple's own iPod Camera Connector, which connects to the bottom of the Pod and provides a USB socket via which you can connect your digital camera. For older iPods (third and fourth generation only), Belkin's Digital Camera Link does a similar thing. And the same company's Media Reader allows you to hook up directly to the memory cards used in digital cameras and other devices.

BELKIN

Car accessories

Several major car manufacturers are now offering built-in iPod connectivity, among them BMV, Volvo, Mercedes and Nissan. But don't worry if you lack a recent high-end vehicle – there are various other options for Podding out your motor:

Complete systems

Models include: **Alpine head units**
with iPod Interface Box
Cost (approx): $350/£250

This is the slickest solution: a car stereo head unit with a jog wheel for directly controlling your iPod and a screen that lets you browse and see what's currently playing. Your Pod is safely stowed in the glove compartment, where it is charged by the car's battery.

Other options

If you don't want the expense and hassle of replacing your current car stereo system, try a cassette adapter – as pictured – or an FM transmitter (see p.206). Either way, the sound

quality, though not perfect, should be good enough for in-car use (especially with better-quality models such as Griffin's SmartDeck, which also lets you control the iPod using the buttons of the car's cassette player).

Also available are power cables for recharging via a cigar-lighter socket, and "holsters" – essentially in-car docks, some of which have power connections and FM transmitters built in.

For more auto iPod solutions visit www.ipodmycar.com

extras

Cases

There are hundreds of iPod cases available, from the water-proof (www.lilipods.com) and seriously protective "iPod Armor" (www.halfkeyboard.com) to the designer (www.gucci.com).

Second skins

Models include: iSkin; Speck Products Silicon Case
Cost (approx): $30/£20

Stretchy iPod skins that do a good job of protecting your Pod from dust, scratches, etc. They also offer a degree of shock-absorbance. They come in loads of colours and iSkin even offers an option of adding customized graphics to your model. It's worth checking to see whether the specific skin you want works with other accessories and the Dock.

Sports cases

Models include: Marware Sportsuit Convertible
Cost (approx): $40/£35

There are loads of sports models on the market that feature either a wrist or armband as well as a standard belt clip, so you can go to the gym, jog, or whatever floats your boat. Marware's case also features an earphone pocket on the flap. Again, be sure that the case you buy doesn't compromise your ability to use the iPod with either the Dock or other accessories.

Travel speakers

Models include: Cube Travel Speakers by Pacific Rim; SRST70 by Sony; iStation by Logic3
Cost (approx): $30–100/£20–50

If you travel with your iPod, a small pair of speakers is great to have. Any powered speakers with a minijack connection will do the job, including those used for computers, but there are many iPod-specific models available, complete with dock connectors. Some will also charge your iPod whilst they play – a very handy feature when away from home for a week or two.

Speakers with their own power source (battery or plug) let the music play longer and louder than those which draw their energy from the iPod. Our favourites are those by Pacific Rim (pictured above), which pleasingly and practically fold away into a cube, and the Logic3 iStation, which has a fantastic sound for its size, folds flat when not being used, and also comes bundled with a nifty remote control.

213

extras

Home speaker units

Models include: SoundDock by Bose; Klipsch iGroove; Apple iPod Hi-Fi
Cost (approx): $90–350/£50–250

An alternative to connecting your Pod
to a hi-fi (see p.129) is a self-contained
iPod speaker system. These are easy to
move from room to room, and they're
also space efficient. A long-standing
favourite in this field is the Bose
SoundDock. At $299/£249, it's
not cheap, but the sound is
exceptionally clear and punchy
for the size, and the remove control
is a welcome extra.

Apple's own home speaker unit, the Apple iPod
Hi-Fi, costs even more (in the US at least), but offers a line input
so you can hook-up a CD or DVD player, AirPort Express or any
other audio device (note that to connect a turntable you'll need a
separate pre-amp). And if you don't mind forking out for enough
batteries to power a small village,
it can be taken out and about
ghettoblaster-
style.

Powered speakers

Models include: **Audioengine 5; Genelec 8030A**
Cost (approx): $350–1200/£200–600

One problem with iPod home speaker units is that they offer no flexibility in terms of stereo separation – unlike with traditional hi-fi speakers, which you can position as far apart as you like. Pairs of powered speakers – aka active speakers – get around this problem. One or both of the speakers contains its own amplifier, so all you need is a source – either an iPod, computer or AirPort Express (see p.132).

The Audioengine 5 stands out as a very neat solution for iPod owners. These 70W per channel speakers feature a USB input up-top for connecting an iPod Dock and around the back there's an auxiliary power socket, so you can plug an AirPort Express straight in. For the price ($250/£200), they sound excellent.

At the top end of the market are Genelec's range of bi-amplified speakers (ie both speakers have an integrated amplifier). These have long been a popular choice for studio use, thanks to their incredibly detailed and rich sound, but they're equally well suited for audiophile home use. Each speaker connects using an XLR cable, so you'll have to get a suitable "splitter" to connect an iPod, but the resulting sound is well worth it.

Earphones

The "earbuds" that come with iPods are decent enough, but they're not exactly hi-fi and they do tend to get fried quite quickly. Also, there's the problem that when you wear them in the street everyone instantly knows what you've got in your pocket. There are thousands of alternatives you could consider (you'll find reviews of loads at www.headphone.com), but the type that are really worth checking out – since you probably use your iPod when out and about in noisy surroundings – are sound-isolating in-ear headphones.

In-ear headphones

Models include: Shure E2c, E3c & E4c; Etymotic ER-series
Cost (approx): $100+/£70+

This kind of earphone sticks right into the ear canal, in the process removing much ambient sound. As a result, not only is the sound much better, but you can listen to music at a much lower volume level, which is better for your ears. There are some relatively cheap models on the market, but if you can afford a bit more, check out the E2c, E3c and E4c models from Shure (a company which made its name manufacturing microphones). The isolation is impressive and the sound even more so. If you have money to burn, another manufacturer worth investigating is Etymotic. Their ER-series headphones produce a stunning sound.

iPod clothes & bags

Models include: SCOTTeVEST; Burton Ronin 2L; Felicidade Groove Bag
Cost (approx): $100+/£75+

If listening to your Pod isn't enough, you could choose to wear it. If you don't mind forking out, there are various clothes and bags with built-in Pod capabilities, such as Burton's Ronin 2L snow-boarding jacket, which features a set of duplicate iPod controls on the sleeve and a specially designed protective pouch. SCOTTeVEST make many high-tech clothes, while Felicidade's Groove Bag is the best-known of the various "beat bags" available.

...and clothes for iPods

Models include: iPod Socks by Apple; iPod Cozies by Chuckles Central
Cost (approx): $20+/£15+

Once you've dressed yourself up in designer iPod clothing it's time to get your Pod ready for the cat-walk. Apple offer a technicolour set of six iPod Socks to help you coordinate, while Chuckles Central's iPod Cozies feature a chunkier stitch and ani-mal faces. They're all good fun but offer little protection – except from frostbite.

217

extras

Wireless remote controls

Models include: Apple Remote; Griffin AirClick
Cost (approx): $29–50/£19–35

If you (a) play your iPod through your hi-fi or TV, and (b) don't like getting out of your chair, you'll like the idea of a wireless iPod remote control. Obviously, it won't allow you to browse, but it will let you access volume, play/pause and previous/next controls from anywhere in the room – or even further afield.

For home use, the ideal option is to combine one of Apple's newer Universal Docks (see p.208) with an Apple Remote (pictured). The latter are available separately, or with new Macs, which can be controlled with the same unit.

Alternatively, try a third-party product such as the Griffin AirClick (pictured). Because they don't require the Dock to function, these can be useful on the move and in the car. The disadvantage is that you can't recharge your Pod or connect to a Dock while using an AirClick with a newer iPod, as your Pod's Dock connector is already occupied by the receiver unit.

The AirClick USB version connects to your computer to offer remote control of iTunes and various other applications.

AirClick

Universal remote control

Models include: **Griffin's Total Remote**
Cost (approx): $25/£15

Here's an ingenious accessory for the technically minded. The idea is to turn your iPod into a remote control for your TV, hi-fi, media centre, or just about anything that is controlled via infrared (IR). This can be achieved with a device such as Griffin's Total Remote, though

The engadget team show how it's done. For a full walk-through, and everything else gadget-related, visit: www.engadget.com

you'll also need a handheld computer with IR capability (and a free weekend) to get everything up and running.

First, use the handheld computer – in conjunction with the Total Remote software – to "sample" the signals from your regular remote controls. Then comes the clever bit: you import these IR "clips" onto your PC or Mac as regular audio files with names such as "TV off", "Hi-fi volume up", etc. This is done using standard sound recording software (see p.136). Next, you import the files into appropriately named iTunes playlists and upload them to your iPod. Plug in the Total Remote device and the job's done.

For a step-by-step guide, visit www.engadget.com and search for "iPod remote control".

extras

iPod Pets

Models include: Sega iDog
Cost (approx): $50/£30

Real dogs may be dependable friends, but they require food and exercise and suffer from bad breath. An altogether more satisfactory canine companion is the iDog – a robotic mutt with built-in speaker that will dance when connected to your iPod (standard minijack cable required). To maximize the depth of your relationship, the iDog will let you know when it's happy via flashing lights and a waggle of its ears and tail. Who said the modern world has lost its way?

24

Extra software

iPod and iTunes self-improvement

If you've ever browsed a software download website and seen the amazing quantity of free and nearly free booty on offer, you won't be surprised to learn that there are scores of extra applications, utilities and plug-ins available for use with iTunes and the iPod. For once, there's more for Mac than PC, but Windows users will still find plenty on offer. We've spotlighted a few useful or interesting things in the next few pages, but there are loads more to be found throughout this book, and on the websites listed on p.246.

extras

iPod to iTunes copying tools

Platform: Mac & PC
Cost: Shareware

There are a number of programs available that will let you copy music from your iPod to a computer – very useful if you want to restore your iTunes Library in the event of your computer dying or being stolen, or if you upgrade to a new machine. You could also use one of these applications to donate the music on your iPod to your friends, though doing so with copyrighted music files will push you onto the wrong side of the law.

iPod.iTunes and iPodRip will both do the job on a Mac, while EphPod is a good choice for PC users. Also worth exploring, and available for both Mac and PC, is PodUtil.

iPod.iTunes www.crispsofties.com
iPodRip www.thelittleappfactory.com
EphPod www.ephpod.com
PodUtil www.kennettnet.co.uk/software

These kinds of applications can also help you perform other syncing tasks with an iPod and iTunes, though bear in mind that they sometimes stop working when you install a new version of iTunes or update your iPod's software.

AppleScripts & Automator

Platform: Mac
Cost: Freeware

AppleScript is a simple programming language that can be used to automate tasks and functions on a Mac. And if your machine is running OS X Tiger (or later) you also have the option of achieving the same end with the in-built Automator application, which offers a non-techie environment for combining "Actions" to create time-saving "Workflows". Hundreds of AppleScripts and Actions have been written for iTunes and iPods and can be downloaded for free. They can do everything from automatically downloading cover art for tracks in your Library, to making it possible to delete song files directly from a playlist. Start here:

Doug's AppleScripts For iTunes www.dougscripts.com
Automator Actions www.apple.com/downloads/macosx/automator

iTunes controllers

Platform: Mac
Cost: Shareware

iTunes controller programs come in many forms and with loads of different features: floating windows, hotkeys, alarm clocks, menu-bar controls, etc. A couple worth checking out are M-Beat, SizzlingKeys and MenuTunes; search the download archives listed on p.248 for many more.

M-Beat www.thelittleappfactory.com
MenuTunes www.ithinksw.com
SizzlingKeys www.yellowmug.com/sk4it

extras

Life2Go & iPodSync

Platform: Mac OS X (Life2Go); Windows XP (iPodSync)
Cost: $12–15

Mentioned elsewhere in this book, Life2Go and iPodSync are tools for automatically loading up your iPod with all sorts of data. They can keep your Pod up to date with unread email, address book and calendar entries, notes/Stickies and bookmarks. And they can download RSS feeds for news, weather, stock market reports, horoscopes and more. Life2Go even provides driving directions. Both programs work by making the most of the iPod's Notes feature (see p.196). With Life2Go, if you use an older Pod that doesn't support Notes, the information is transferred into the Contacts folder.

Life2Go and iPodSync can also manage file back-ups and Podcasts (see p.164). For more, see:

iPodSync www.ipod-sync.com (PC)
Life2Go www.kainjow.com/life2go (Mac)

iPod icons

Platform: Mac (some PC available)
Cost: Free

OK, they're not exactly extra programs, but anyone who wants to turn their computer into an iPod shrine might be interested in the free icon families – including many devoted to Pods – available from sites such as:

IconFactory www.iconfactory.com (Mac)
InterfaceLIFT www.interfacelift.com (PC & Mac)

To change the icon of a file or folder on a Mac, choose an icon that you've downloaded, single-click it and press Apple+C (copy). Then select the file or folder on which you want to use it and press Apple+I to bring up the Show Info box. Click the current icon at the top of the box and press Apple+V (paste) to overwrite it with the new one; you can also get rid of it later by clicking it here and pressing backspace.

If you can't find a Mac icon that does your Pod justice, download Pic2Icon (www.sugarcubesoftware.com) and make your own.

Hacking the iPod's icons

Assuming you don't mind nullifying your Apple warranty (or even permanently damaging your Pod) and you are reasonably technically minded, you could try customizing the icons, fonts and other elements on your iPod's screen. For the full story, read the article found here:
www.ilounge.com/index.php/articles/comments
/beginners-guide-to-changing-ipod-graphics

extras

Album artwork

Platform: Mac & PC
Cost: Free

There are numerous scripts, websites and applications to be found online to help you harvest album artwork and load it into iTunes. For example:

iTunesArtImporter yvg.com/itunesartimporter.shtml (PC)
Art4iTunes art4itunes.com (PC & Mac)

Once you've filled your library with artwork, we seriously recommend you get your paws on CoverFlow. This slick-looking little application for Macs running OS X Tiger lets you scroll through your iTunes library, album cover by album cover, in an environment reminiscent of iChat's video conferencing screen. Once you've found what you want to listen to, double-clicking the cover sets it playing in iTunes.

CoverFlow www.steelskies.com/coverflow

SonicSwap & myTunes

Platform: Mac & PC
Cost: Free

myTunes is an all-singing-and-dancing tool that enables you to share playlists with friends on the SonicSwap network (which has over 50,000 members) and add playlists from others who have similar music collections. There's no actual file sharing going on (so it's all perfectly legal), just loads of list sharing. As well as this primary networking feature, the application lets you download cover art for the music in your iTunes library and also track down discographies and lyrics for your favourite artists.

Mytunes www.sonicswap.com/mytunes

extras

And a few more...

iEatBrainz homepage.com/jbtule Cost: Free

Uses the "sound" of a song to search for its artist details within the MusicBrainz online database. Useful if Gracenote fails you.

BPM Inspector blacktree.com/apps/iTunes-BPM Cost: Shareware

Clever little floating application that lets you determine the bpm of a song by tapping along to the beat.

Ear Mail www.newton-eig.com Cost: $50

Listen to your emails on your iPod.

webRemote www.deadendsw.com Cost: Shareware

Control iTunes using any Web browser.

PodQuest www.mibasoft.dk Cost: $10

Download MapQuest driving instructions to your iPod.

LED Spectrum Analyser www.maczoop.com Cost: Shareware

A visualizer program that emulates a spectrum analyser.

ListSaver www.deadendsw.com Cost: Shareware

Back up and restore iTunes playlists.

DotPod www.dotpod.net Cost: Shareware

Make music available over the Internet from your iPod (only legal with uncopyrighted music).

iBrew www.dropcap.co.uk/ibrew Cost: Free

Allows your iPod to connect with a regular teapot to test the strength and temperature of your cuppa-to-be.

First aid ✚

25

Backing up

keeping your music safe

Just like any other computer file, music files can be deleted or damaged. Hard drives die, and computers get stolen, damaged or destroyed. As we've seen (see p.222), with the right software it's perfectly possible to recover music from your iPod back to your computer. However, if you have more music on your computer than your Pod, or if you regularly carry your laptop and Pod around in the same bag, it's definitely worth having a back-up copy of your archive.

Backing up your iTunes Library

Backing up iTunes properly is not simply a matter of duplicating the actual song files: you need to create a copy of the whole iTunes folder (found in Music, within your Home folder, on a Mac, and in My Music on a PC), which contains not only the songs but also a record of all your playlists, preferences, etc, in two databases, named something like "iTunes Music Library.xml" and "iTunes 4 Music Library".

Ideally, you should copy the folder to an external media, the most obvious examples being external hard drives and optical discs (CD and DVD). You could back up instead to a separate folder or partition on your hard drive, but if your computer is stolen or the drive damaged, you lose both your original and back-up copy.

Backing up to an external drive

The most convenient way to back up your iTunes folder is to drag a copy to an external drive that can be kept completely separate from your computer. Such drives are relatively cheap (considering how much woe they can save you from), are very easy to use, and are more than capacious enough to do the job. With an external hard drive you can copy everything in one go and, should the worst happen, restoring your iTunes folder is easy.

Consolidate Library...

By selecting Consolidate Library from the iTunes Advanced menu, iTunes scans your system for music files and then copies them all to your Library. You could then search for and delete the originals using either your OS X or Windows search functions. Try to do this prior to moving your Library to a new machine or backing it up to an external drive (see above).

To restore a lost Library, first open iTunes Preferences and in the Advanced pane check both boxes that relate to the iTunes folder. Then quit iTunes and drag the whole back-up iTunes folder from the hard drive to its original location, replacing the existing iTunes Music folder if asked. Now relaunch iTunes and your Library, playlists and preferences should have been recreated.

Backing up to DVD or CD

If you don't want to buy an external hard drive but already have either a CD or DVD burner, then you can use this as a means of backing up your song files. CDs are not ideal, because of their relatively small capacity, but DVDs are great (you should be able to fit the equivalent of around 150 audio CDs on a single DVDR).

First, create a new playlist and drag your Library icon (or whatever you want to back up) onto it in the Source List. Next, open Preferences and under Burning choose to create a data DVD (or CD). Close Preferences, select the playlist, and hit the Burn button in the top right of the iTunes window. Assuming your Library is pretty large, iTunes will not be able to fit all the songs on a single disc. When iTunes has burned what it can to the first disc, it will prompt you to insert subsequent discs until the job is done.

To restore these song files, drag them from the optical discs into the open iTunes window (dropping them either on the Song List or on specific playlist icons if required). This will prompt iTunes to copy them to the iTunes Music folder.

> **TIP:** You will additionally need to locate your iTunes Library file and back it up separately in order to save your playlists. It is easily restored by simply dragging the back-up copy into the iTunes folder.

Back up with Backup

OS X users who sign up for a .Mac account gain access to an Apple program called Backup, which can be used to copy your files to either an optical disc, external hard drive or even remote server (.Mac also provides you with an online backup drive called iDisk). For more details, see: www.mac.com

Incremental backups

A backup is much more useful if it is kept up to date. If you are using an external hard drive, simply copy the iTunes folder onto the drive once every few weeks or so and replace the backed-up one. Alternatively, use a third-party application (see below) to synchronize your iTunes folder and the external drive's version.

If you are using the burning-playlists method, here's a little trick to help you keep track of what's changed in your Library in the time since your last backup. Create a new Smart Playlist (see p.71) that only features songs added after the date that you backed up. When you next feel the need to create a backup DVD, simply burn this Smart Playlist and then change its parameters to feature only songs added from that date.

Utilities

Check the software archives listed on p.248 for backing up utilities, or go straight to Anapod:

Anapod www.redchairsoftware.com/anapod/ctable.php

> ▶ TIP: If you want to back up important files and folders
> from your Mac to your iPod, the task is made simple
> by the application Life2Go (see p.224), which will keep
> selected folders backed up every time you sync.

26

Help!

troubleshooting & maintenance

Despite the minimalist design of the iPod, and the intuitive look and feel of iTunes, both can throw the occasional curve ball. There are a million and one things that might be the cause of your woes – and we simply don't have the room in a book of this size to cover all of them. However, this chapter does provide answers to many of the most common iPod and iTunes problems – as well as tips on maximizing your iPod's battery life. As for the rest, there's always the Internet, so if you don't find the help you need here, turn to p.247 for a list of online resources.

iPod ailments

Just like regular computers, iPods sometimes crash, freeze up, or generally start behaving like belligerent two-year-olds. This is most commonly the fault of a software glitch and, when it happens, you can usually solve the problem by resetting your Pod or, if that fails, updating your iPod software.

Resetting an iPod

To reset your iPod (this won't delete your music, files or preferences) hold down the following key combination for around ten seconds, until the Apple logo appears:

Menu & **Select** (all iPod models with a click wheel)
▶II & **Menu** (third generation iPods)

If this doesn't seem to have any effect, try connecting the Pod to its power supply, toggling the Hold switch on and off, and then resetting again.

Updating and restoring

First, make sure you have the most recent versions of iTunes and the iPod Updater. You can do this by visiting www.apple.com/ipod/download (or, on a Mac, by running Software Update from the Apple menu). When you run iPod Updater it should offer you two choices: Update, which adds the latest software to your Pod; and Restore, which returns the device to its factory state, removing all music (don't worry, it will still be there in iTunes), files and settings. You

Included iPod Software Updates

iPod shuffle Software 1.0
- iPod shuffle

iPod Software 3.0.2
- Click Wheel iPod

iPod mini Software 1.2
- iPod mini

iPod photo Software 1.0
- iPod photo

iPod Software 2.2
- iPod with dock connector

iPod software 1.4
- Touch Wheel iPod
- Scroll Wheel iPod

Interpreting the iPod's icons

 If your iPod suspects that there might be an issue with its hard drive, it will automatically start to run its in-built disk scan utility. The screen will display a disk and magnifying-glass icon while the scan is under way (this can take around twenty minutes). When the scan is complete, you will be presented with an icon.

 ▶ **Everything's OK** You have nothing to worry about – your hard drive is in perfect condition.

 ▶ **Scan failed** The scan has failed and will be repeated next time you turn on your iPod. You can force it to restart by resetting it (see opposite).

 ▶ **Scan found issues** The scan has found problems on the hard drive. If you see this icon you need to restore your iPod using the latest iPod Updater (see opposite).

 ▶ **Sad iPod icon** This is not good news – your iPod may need to be sent away for repair (see p.239). But try restoring with the latest iPod software first (see opposite).

Other iPod icons you may encounter include:

 ▶ **iPod software problem** Try resetting and then restoring the Pod (see opposite). Still no joy? It could be physically damaged, in which case you may need to send it to Apple for repair (see p.239).

 ▶ **Low battery** This one's pretty obvious: you need a recharge. But if it's appearing more frequently that you'd expect, you may need to replace the battery. For more on this – and tips for maximizing battery life – see p.240

might want to try Update first, and then Restore if that doesn't solve the problem. Then launch iTunes to put your music back onto the Pod.

first aid

My iPod doesn't appear when I plug it in

Most iPod owners have come across this problem once or twice. Try the following:

▶ **Reset the Pod** See p.236.

▶ **Empty your Trash and restart your computer** A software glitch or a full hard drive can stop Mac OS X recognizing attached drives.

▶ **Force-mount** If iTunes sees the iPod but it won't work as a hard drive, even though Disk Use is enabled (see p.172), try forcing it to "mount". Reset the Pod (see p.236) and, at the Apple logo screen, hold **Select** and ▶II (on any iPod with a click wheel) or ◀◀ and ▶▶I (third generation iPods).

▶ **Update your iPod software** See p.236.

▶ **Delete iPodDriver.kext** On a Mac, this rogue file can stop iTunes and the iPod Updater software recognizing a Pod (see below).

Killing iPodDriver.kext

In Mac OS X 10.3 or later
▶ In Finder go to System/Library/Extensions and trash the iPodDriver.kext file.
▶ Download the latest Mac OS X Combined Update by running Software Update from the Apple menu, while connected to the Internet.
▶ Restart the computer when prompted and then connect the iPod.

Mac OS X 10.2.8 and earlier
▶ Open Terminal from Utilities (in Applications).
▶ Carefully type:
sudo rm -R /System/Library/Extensions/iPodDriver.kext
▶ Hit Return on your keyboard and enter your administrator password when prompted.
▶ Quit Terminal, restart your Mac, install the latest version of iTunes (see p.40). Then restart again and connect your iPod.

The display is in the wrong language

To get back to English, first hit the Menu button a few times to reach the top-level menu. Then select the third item from the bottom – this is always Settings. In the next menu, again select the third item up (always Language) and then choose English.

Look online...

If your Pod is still not behaving – and you've tried everything obvious, such as plugging it in to recharge and making sure the Hold switch isn't on (see p.62) – then search online for help. Google (including groups.google.com) is a good place to start, but also try Apple's own Net discussion area (discussions.info.apple. com) and the iPod supersites listed on p.246.

Diagnostic mode

It is possible to run various tests on an iPod in Diagnostic Mode, which is entered by resetting the Pod and then, when the Apple logo appears, pressing ◄◄, ►► and **Select** until you hear a little chirp, at which point a new menu should appear. The tests are very techie, and not really designed for consumer use. So if you do want to explore this mode, be sure to read up on the subject online before you start. A good place to start is www.ipoding.com

---

Sending an iPod for repair

If all else fails, you'll need to send your Pod to meet its maker. Repair can be arranged via an Apple retail store, but you may have to make an appointment in advance. Alternatively, Apple will mail you a box in which you can post the Pod back to them. You can arrange this online (depot.info.apple.com/ipod) or by phone on 1-800-275-2273 (US) or 0870-8760-753 (UK). Either way, you'll need to provide your Pod's serial number – which you'll find on the back of the device in tiny print.

first aid

Battery issues

There has been much controversy about the overall life span of the iPod battery (see p.14) and the speed with which it runs down when being used. Recent models have improved the situation, but it's still worth bearing in mind the following.

To maximize the listening time from a single battery charge:

▶ Make sure your iPod software is up to date (see p.236).

▶ Avoid using the backlight, and turn off the clock and calendar alarm functions. While you're at it, turn the Clicker off.

▶ Use lower-quality song files (see p.111) – the iPod doesn't have to work so hard to play them. And try not to use the ◀◀ and ▶▶ buttons too frequently, as they require more hard-drive use.

▶ Use the Hold switch so that your iPod doesn't sing to itself in your pocket when buttons get pressed accidentally.

To extend the battery's overall life span:

▶ Plug it in as much as possible, but let it run down completely around once a month.

▶ Use your iPod regularly.

▶ Avoid exposing a Pod to extremes of temperature.

Dead batteries

If your iPod battery does eventually run out of steam, either: send the Pod to Apple for a replacement (this will be free if your warranty hasn't expired); get a company such as iPodResQ or PlugStore to come to your aid; or do it yourself, by buying a new battery and downloading instructions from a company such as iPodBattery.com or iPod Mini Batteries (not just for iPod minis!):

Service & Support www.apple.com/support/ipod
iPodBattery.com www.ipodbattery.com (US)
iPodResQ www.ipodresq.com (US)
iPod Mini Batteries www.ipodminibattery.com (UK)
PlugStore www.plugstore.net (UK)

Problems in iTunes

For iTunes troubleshooting advice relating to burning CDs and DVDs, see p.99. And for problems playing music, see p.85. Following are a few other common iTunes problems.

I've run out of disk space on my computer

First of all, clean up your iTunes Library. Sort the songs by file size (see p.92) and either delete any unwanted uncompressed files (AIFFs, WAVs or Apple Lossless) or convert them to something more space-efficient (see p.119). Next look at your system as a whole and see if you can save any space by deleting, or archiving, old files and disposing of temporary files. Finally, consider getting an extra hard drive (see p.11).

The text in my Song List looks garbled

This is most likely caused by problems with your ID3 tags (special bits of code within music files that record the track information that you see when you are browsing your iTunes Library). The problem should be easily solved: in the Song List, select the tracks causing you grief and choose Convert ID3 Tags... from the iTunes Advanced menu.

iTunes says my Library file is invalid

Within your iTunes folder, along with the actual music folders, you should find an iTunes Library file – a database document that records where your music files are as well as data such as playlists, play counts, etc. If your Library file is missing or corrupt, you could replace it with a backed up version, if you ever made one (see p.231). If not, you could use a program such as iPodRip (see p.222) to restore the information from your iPod to iTunes. Or you could try dragging your iTunes Music folder (see p.51) to the Library icon in iTunes' Source List. This should bring back all the songs, but not playlists, play counts and other information.

You may also run into this problem if you've moved your music archive to somewhere other than the default location. In this case, specify the new location via the Advanced tab in Preferences.

Still struggling?

Upgrade to the most recent version of iTunes (see p.40). Or, if you're already up to date, uninstall and reinstall your current version. But, if at all possible, back up first (see p.231).

Dead computers, new computers

If your computer dies or gets stolen, you can – once you have a new one – either restore your music archive from a backup, if you made one (see p.231), or download a program that lets you copy the music from your iPod to your computer (see p.224). Whatever you do, don't sync your iPod with the new computer's empty iTunes Library – you'll lose everything.

If you upgrade your computer, the same options apply. Or you could copy the files from the old computer to the new one as described on p.106.

iPodology

iPods
online

websites and blogs

I f you want to find out more about any of the subjects
covered in this book – or track down that ellusive iPod
accessory, join a forum or download the latest iTunes
plug-ins – you're going to have to hit the Web. There's
an almost frightening number of iPod and iTunes sites
out there, including comprehensive Pod portals, with
discussion forums, troubleshooting tips, news and reviews.
Apple's own site is also a useful resource, and there are
even a number of iPod blogs (weblogs). Following are the
pick of the bunch; for online Pod weirdness, turn to p.249.

iPodology

iPod sites and forums

iLounge www.ilounge.com
Everything iPod www.everythingipod.com
iPoding www.ipoding.com
iPods-Mini-iPods www.ipods-mini-ipod.com
iPod Studio ipodstudio.com

Apple

Home www.apple.com
iTunes/iPod home www.apple.com/music
Apple Store www.apple.com/store
Apple Discussions discussions.info.apple.com
Software Updates www.apple.com/support/downloads
Service & Support www.apple.com/support/ipod

Help, hacks and maintenance

Apple www.info.apple.com/usen/ipod/tshoot.html
Chipmunk www.chipmunk.nl/iPod
iPod Hacks www.ipodhacks.com
MacFixit www.macfixit.com

Buying and accessories

Amazon www.amazon.com
Apple Store www.apple.com/store
Everything iPod www.everythingipod.com
Griffin www.griffintechnology.com
ilounge www.iLounge.com/loungestore.php

Software downloads

About macs.about.com/cs/itunes/a/itunes_utils.htm
Doug's AppleScripts www.dougscripts.com/itunes
iLounge www.ilounge.com/downloads.php
iPodSoft www.ipodsoft.com
LittleAppFactory www.thelittleappfactory.com
TuCows www.tucows.com

iPod blogs

BlogFreaks ipod.blogfreaks.com
iPod News www.ipod-news.blogspot.com
MyiPodBlog myipodblog.blogspot.com
The iPod Blog www.theipodblog.com

And more...

For an overview of what the iPod is, who made it happen and how it's changed over the years, visit the relevant pages of Wikipedia, starting with:

Wikipedia en.wikipedia.org/wiki/IPod

If you have a suggestion about how the iPod could be improved, then tell Apple at:

iPod Feedback www.apple.com/feedback/ipod.html

When you don't get a personal reply, become an enemy of the iPod state, at:

Anti-iPod www.anti-ipod.co.uk

iP*odd*

stranger than fiction

I t is, without a doubt, a weird world, and there's nothing quite like music, gadgets and fads to bring the crackpots out of the woodwork. What follows are a few dispatches from the people who put the odd in the Pod.

Engravings from hell

What not to get engraved on your little shiny friend:
www.ipodlaughs.com/ipod/iengraver
www.methodshop.com/mp3/articles/iPodEngraving
www.ipodlaughs.com/ipod/ipocalypse/disturbingengravings.asp

And, if you want the T-shirt, visit…
www.cafeshops.com/ipod_laughs

Linux on iPod

Bored of playing music? Why not use your iPod as a platform for a UNIX-clone operating system?

iPod health warnings

Love your Pod a little too much? Be cured here:
www.theregister.co.uk/2005/05/20/ipod_health_warnings/

Photo galleries

What do you get if you cross an iPod with Photoshop?
www.ipodlaughs.com/ipod/ipocalypse

And for shots of globetrotting Pods:
gallery.ilounge.com

A close shave…

iShave
Rocken Sie nicht unrasiert!

Hochkarätige Schertechnologie

Ein Y-geometrischer Scherkopf garantiert eine glatte und hautfreundliche Rasur. Kombiniert mit dem hochwertigen Scherkopf-Schwingsystem erfasst der iShave durch das 6-fach System mehr Barthaare in weniger Zügen, d.h. sie haben noch vor Ende des Liedes eine glatte und sanft rasierte Haut.

A hoax, perhaps, but also one of the best ideas since sliced bread

251

Apple-ad-meets-Microsoft-man magic moment

Pod users who have seen the widely circulated videos of Microsoft's Steve Ballmer (www.ntk.net/ballmer), will love this reworking: www.macboy.com/cartoons/ballmer

iPod open mic

This London club night invites you to bring your own music – fifteen minutes on stage to show what your Pod can do…

Playlist www.ipod-dj.com

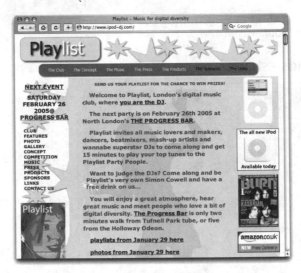

iGod

Or if you prefer divine inspiration to club perspiration, you're going to need this:

BiblePod www.kainjow.com/?xml/software/biblepod.xml

Pod DIY

If money is an issue, there are always the rather special
paper iPod alternatives, which can be found at
homepage.mac.com/colinbaxter/ipod/ipodclick.html

From sickjokes.net, here's a very easy way
to transform your iPod an iPod shuffle,
using only a humble Post-it note

> **TIP:** If you don't like the backlight colour of your iPod's
> screen and, on third generation models, the buttons
> – and you don't mind voiding your warranty – try
> something in blue, green or orange. Visit: www.ipodmods.com

Check this out... www.gizmodo.com/images/bizzaro_ipod.mov

Dock crazy

Is it a bird? Is it a plane? No, it's a log? ... with legs and speakers and an iPod dock up-top.

Storylog
www.housespecial.org
/products/storylog.htm

Not big enough for you? Then why not turn your boudoir into an iPod haven with Pause – "the World's First iPod Compatible Bed". And to add extra spice to your iPod bedroom, there's always iBuzz, the Pod-friendly musical orgasm machine.

Pause www.designmobel.co.nz/pause.html
iBuzz www.ibuzz.co.uk

iBuzz The music-activated orgasm machine!

iBuzz Music Activated Sex Toy

Works with any MP3 player or portable music device!

※ Bullet vibrates in time to your music!
※ Turn the music up for stronger vibrations!
※ Stimulating fun for him and her!
※ Easy to use - plug in and play!
※ Works with or without music!

Only £29.99!
Enter quantity: 1   Add to basket

Now available in the US! Click here for iBuzz USA.

iPod-megaphone-helmet

Great for selling ice-creams, and more likely to get you noticed at a party than turning up with an Apple iPod Hi-Fi (see p.214). For full instructions on how to pimp your own helmet, visit: www.instructables.com

Fancy dress

iPod fancy dress can be approached from both directions – either you dress up (right), or your Pod does (below).

iAttire www.iattire.net

Larry Koteff made this wonderful iPod costume in 2003.

iPodology

Bricking it

Who needs a Dock when all the raw materials are sitting at the back of the toy cupboard?

flickr.com/photos/linuxmatt/sets

In fact, who needs an iPod at all when you have Lego?

PodBrix www.podbrix.com

Here's one Peter made earlier...

Index

Index